D1519512

VULNERABLE
AND
VICTORIOUS

My hope is that my experiences of where I've been can help people find the full life they've been looking for.

To my family and friends for believing and being available along my journey of vulnerability. You've been an incredible example to follow!

CONTENTS

CHAPTER ONE

REALITY UNDER THE RUG
THE SPILL AND THE SHAME

I didn't mean for what happened that disastrous day to actually happen. I felt like my life was flashing right before my very eyes. I had to come up with some type of plan to cover up the carnage of clumsiness and carelessness staring back at me, reminding me of what I knew I wasn't supposed to do. I quickly began to move our living room rug over the fruit punch-stained section of my mom's pristine white carpeting, hoping that I would be able to cover up both my choices and the eventual consequences that I believed at that moment would keep me from ever having a normal childhood. As I stared at the juice-splattered crime-scene-looking stain on the carpet, I could hear my mom's voice replaying the rules in my head.

We had one rule in the house that was voiced very loud and clear for as long as we lived in the house, and it was that there was no food or drink allowed in the living room. (Which to me never totally made sense. I mean this was called a "living room" and what better way to live than to have your favorite food and drinks with you!) Now, of course, we were able to bring some snacks in every now and then for family movie nights, but other than that, the living room was a sacred space for nothing to be snuck into it. A space that was carefully decorated and arranged with my mom's fancy furniture, fine ornaments, and carousel collections. I remember covering the red Kool-Aid drenched carpet and running to my room, praying that the carpet would absorb the juice before my mom would bust through my bedroom door like the Kool-Aid man and call out my full name upon what she would discover. Well, as you probably have experienced when you tried to come up with a strategy to dodge punishment as a kid, the parents usually win. I knew it was only a matter of time before I was going to hear my full name called out by my mom, and I would have to ultimately come clean and serve my sentence, but not before an attempt to escape.

A FALL FROM FULL LIFE

Maybe you can feel my pain if you've experienced this type of paralyzing moment as a kid at some point in your life. You knew you shouldn't have done it, and you were horrified at the thought of being found out, so you came up with what seemed like a fool-proof plan. You can try to cover and conceal as much as you want to, but it never changes the fact that it still happened and that you are probably in for an inevitable "fall" moment. And that fall, more times than not, keeps us from a life that is full. As John 10:10 says,

"The thief comes only to steal and kill and destroy; I have come that they may have life, and have it to the full."

Now I'm sure this verse wasn't talking about a thief in the form of red Kool-Aid that was coming to steal, kill, and destroy both our family carpet and, more importantly, my life. But we know what it's like to have the thief try and break in and take from us. If you've ever thought of a thief, I'm sure you think of someone dressed in all black with a ski mask that throws a rock through a window or picks a lock to come in and take what is most valuable. Maybe he is a very strategic thief who stands on the roof of an art gallery and is ready to drop in past maximum-security lasers, open up a glass case, and reveal a prized and sophisticated piece of art. The thief has a way about him in that he doesn't take anything right in front of you, but usually manages to take it when you least expect it. And no matter what type of thief you may be dealing with, one thing remains the same: the thief only comes to take what is important. The exception of this thief from the classic thief I just mentioned is that the thief that takes from us is one that we often invite in!

Can you imagine opening the front door to a thief and letting him stroll in and take what he wants? As crazy as it sounds and as much as we don't want to do it, we find ourselves doing it more than we wish we did. Our sin often crouches at the door waiting for it to be unlocked so the thief can come in and to begin to take away what is most valuable to us. The truth is that we know that the thief comes seeking to steal, kill, and destroy, but he can't do what he does if we don't let him. We figure that we have power and control over situations that happen in our lives. The thief usually shows up at the front door, ready to take from us the moment we think we know how to have the power to live full lives. Let's go back to the garden to see how this all began in a moment with Adam and Eve.

THE FIRST FALL

"Now the serpent was more crafty than any of the wild animals the LORD God had made. He said to the woman, "Did God really say, 'You must not eat from any tree in the garden'?" 2 The woman said to the serpent, "We may eat fruit from the trees in the garden, 3 but God did say, 'You must not eat fruit from the tree that is in the middle of the garden, and you must not touch it, or you will die.'" 4 "You will not certainly die," the serpent said to the woman. 5 "For God knows that when you eat from it your eyes will be opened, and you will be like God, knowing good and evil."6 When the woman saw that the fruit of the tree was good for food and pleasing to the eye, and also desirable for gaining wisdom, she took some and ate it. She also gave some to her husband, who was with her, and he ate it" Genesis 3:1-7.

The thief comes in the form of a serpent, and convinces Adam and Eve to believe they know how to live full lives better. A decision of disobedience later, and we are still feeling the experience of those consequences today. Nothing tells us that the serpent has authority, but he is crafty. When the enemy comes and is crafty, it's easy sometimes to be convinced to a freedom that does not actually exist. He works by making us cast doubt and convincing us to become curious to the idea that we might know better through making us false promises that we think will lead to a full life. To make us question and doubt if God is really good by exaggerating His expectations. If you jump back one more chapter, here's what was really said.

"And the LORD God commanded the man, "You are free to eat from any tree in the garden; 17 but you must not eat from the tree of the knowledge of good and evil, for when you eat from it you will certainly die" Genesis 2:16-17.

Not only did God not say that they couldn't eat, but they were commanded to be free to eat! Up until that point, there was the full experience of faith, freedom, a future, and soon-to-be friendship. There was access to more than they could have ever imagined. I always thought it was weird to all of a sudden throw in a rule that there was one tree that could not be eaten from. It almost felt like God was tempting us into sin. The tree wasn't some kind of weird trick or temptation, but a representation of the ability to have free will in deciding to be vulnerable and have a relationship.

I have been married going on four years, and while still being considered a rookie in the marriage world, I do know that spending time with my wife is a key building block. In order to become close to someone, you have to spend time with them. And as you spend that time talking, opening up over coffee, or even simply just chatting about our day and daily mundane tasks together, you ultimately become closer. You become closer not through what you are doing but who you are choosing.

God has a desire to be close to us but won't force it on us; instead it leads to a choice made by us. Choosing God is choosing vulnerability, and that vulnerability leads to closer intimacy and growing with Him relationally. It's amazing how one question could move a commandment into confusion. Confusion moves you to question everything you know, whether it was told to you or not. To make you think it's possible that your will could produce something free. Our confusion adds thoughts in our head and words out of our mouth that tighten up restrictions that weren't there in the first place, which makes us feel like we have permission to test out the fruit to see how good it tastes because we know there's absolutely no way anything wrong could happen, right?

THREE WORDS

There are three words I'm one hundred percent sure you have heard at least once in your lifetime. You most likely heard it when you were a kid when you were at the peak of your curiosity and ready to touch the kitchen stove. You've seen signs with these words posted up all over museums, zoos, and on electric fences in shady warehouse facilities in rural areas in the middle of the night with lightning strikes in the sky. These words often get added to areas where danger is present. For some of you, it was the words that actually led you to even more wanting to do what was clearly stated not to do.

DO NOT TOUCH

Every living, breathing human being has heard these words. Believe it or not, it's the words that God didn't say, but the words that Eve added to the command to not eat from the tree in the middle of the garden.

But God did say, "You must not eat fruit from the tree that is in the middle of the garden, and you must not touch it, or you will die."

So what's up with the added expectation? Isn't it hard enough to not want to take a bite of the fruit, and now we are concerned about not even getting near it and touching it? For some of us, we would say, "Bravo, Eve! Props to you for not even wanting to get close to it!" But have you ever been in a moment where you are working hard to try to talk yourself out of sin before? That internal voice in your head can very quickly trick us into trying to talk us into an open door for inviting sin inside. Sometimes we will actually add expectations to open the door to justify our decisions.

Our focus isn't on what we were told not to do, but

we motivate and negotiate how close we can get before any type of trouble might happen. If I grab ahold of it, I'll most likely cave to it, but if I only look at it, I'm safe, right? I'll head to the party, but I just won't participate. I'll hop online late at night, but not for that long. I'll look at what happens if I change a couple of numbers on my taxes, but I won't actually change them.

The focus isn't about tasting anymore but about touching, which we believe gives us permission to participate. We lose sight of what was commanded and, through our own knowledge, convince our own commitment. We begin to give ourselves reasons why it might be okay, hoping that might lead us to think we were right all along. That it will bring the excitement of new-found knowledge and power. It's usually at that moment that we know we are committed.

The thief comes in very inconspicuously. He twists and turns until he takes and, before we know it, we look around wondering where our peace and joy went, and leaves us feeling like all that is left behind is a mess for us to feel like we have to figure out alone. What we thought we would get isn't what we end up having. Adam and Eve find out that while the food was probably pretty good and made them full (I mean, we are talking fresh from the garden of Eden), nothing from that tree was good enough for the fall they were about to experience.

The thief only comes to try and convince us that he has taken our victory while leaving us with tasting defeat and the reminder of our stains. He likes to not only show us what he has done, but even more likes to tell us who we are after all of what he's taken. That we only have as much of a future as what we see in front of us. Unfortunately, after all this happens, we look around at how we got here, and it's easy for guilt and shame to begin to settle in. We never thought that this much would be taken from us and wish that we would have kept the door of our lives secured. We begin to hide and close us off from those who love us and want to be close to us.

Sometimes the most difficult thing that we face in the midst of all of what we feel has been taken from us is that we decide that nothing can be done. The thief can't tell you what to do; he can only try to convince you of what you should give up. The thief comes seeking to steal, kill and destroy, but can't do what he does if we don't let him. It's time to stop the thief from thieving.

FULL AFTER A FALL

We've all, at one point, kept the door unlocked and let sin in. So what happens after the thief gets in? What happens when we look around and can't see past the guilt and shame that's right in front of us? Most of us probably deal with our decisions like the way I did the moment I witnessed the Kool-Aid hit the carpet. We think and look back to just moments before we let that door open, wondering what we were possibly thinking, letting something like this happen. Just like with Adam and Eve, there's a second temptation that often shows up for us, too, in the moments when we realize our pain, and that is to cover and conceal. We run to where we think it will be safe, separate ourselves, and begin to come up with scenarios to conceal what is real. We try to run away from sin after the sin already happened and push the blame onto someone or something else, in hopes to clear our name. We hope that God doesn't see just how much the thief managed to take. Just as we get ready to think we have it all figured out with crisis and consequence averted, our name gets called.

There were very few moments as a kid growing up in Wisconsin that I managed to get myself in a heap of trouble. I wasn't the kid who pushed the envelope or snuck out of my bedroom window late at night. My mom also had that way about her when she knew something was up. You know the way a lot of moms do. (It's like a radar for moms—"mom-dar.") So you can imagine that when my mom used my full name, I knew we weren't exactly preparing for a great mother-son bonding moment. I came in with a little extra padding on my backside and tears from the fact that I was reminded of what my middle name was and made my way to the scene of the crime. I was fully expecting my mom to replay the rules to me about this being the exact reason why we don't bring food or drink in the living room, but what I got was incredibly different than what I thought.

As I walked into the living room, having heard my full name called, I expected to come in ready to receive my punishment and serve my time. So you can imagine my surprise when I walked in with the rug peeled back with the stain exposed that instead of throwing punishment at me immediately, she simply asked me, "Why didn't you just tell me?"

I was able to come up with plenty of reasons in my mind for why I didn't want to tell her. Ever had expectations of what would you thought the outcome would look like? It's terrifying. You pretty much put a sentence over yourself before anything has even happened. And most of the time, it's those very thoughts that fuel your reason for not wanting to be honest and vulnerable. But whenever you think of the worst-case scenario and end up with something better than what you thought, it ends up being pretty relieving. It's like holding your breath for the longest time to finally be able to exhale and let that breath out. Most of my reasons for not wanting to tell her what happened were really not about what happened or what my consequence would be, but more about how I thought my relationship would be affected.

I realized at that moment that my mom wasn't as concerned about what was on the carpet as much as she was concerned about what was going on in my heart. It could have been really easy for her to only be concerned about what was right (I mean, she loved this carpet), but instead, my relationship and closeness to her were much more important. The hurt I felt in the words she said was knowing that she cared more for me than what I saw on the carpet. Realizing a relationship is the moment that allows you the freedom to finally exhale and let the breath of what you've tried so hard to keep in finally come out. That everything you worked hard to keep in can be healed. That everything you fought so hard to try and control can be traded in for freedom. That everything you felt like you failed with can be forgiven.

Jesus is the same way.

"For the Son of Man came to seek and to save the lost"
Luke 19:10.

Jesus has this deep desire for us to be vulnerable and have victory. His mission isn't to destroy you but to defend you. We know this because He voluntarily took on humanity and became vulnerable, not to sin, but to experience temptation, pain, rejection, and death, for the sake of coming to find those who are lost and bringing them to a place of victory. He doesn't just seek us out and notice us but chooses to be present and walk us through our lostness.

Raise your hand if you like being lost. I can't see any of you at the moment, and I don't know how many are reading this book, but I imagine that none of you are raising your hands right now. As much as we don't like being lost, it doesn't mean that we haven't been or felt lost at different points in our lives. We've made decisions that left us feeling lost, taken wrong turns, had a relationship break, broke up a relationship, hurt others, been hurt by others, hurt ourselves, and the list goes on and on. Even though we may feel or don't know how we managed to get this lost, we have the choice not to stay lost.

I have to admit I am terrible with directions. (More

on that in the coming chapters.) Getting lost for me would be a daily routine, and there would probably be missing signs out for me if I didn't have navigation. But step by step, my navigation manages to get me to my destination as it calls us each, calculating step by step. And even if I manage to make a wrong turn or end up driving down the wrong side of a one-way street, I'm calmly redirected to get back on the right track. When it comes to your life, all you need to do is listen to the voice that is calling out your name and calmly redirecting you step by step.

FORWARD TOWARDS FULL

Jesus calls us and brings us to Himself with the desire that we will be vulnerable and simply come and tell Him everything. Telling Him everything may mean that we will be redirected back to drive through some of the places that remind us of pain, but just like any good navigation, He will get us there. He isn't just interested in calling out to us but also in loving us through. That through telling him, we can rid ourselves of the heaviness that comes from trying to cover up what has happened and begin to find direction, freedom, and a future again.

The thief can confuse us into believing that we matter only based on what we do or don't do, more than realizing we matter already because of who we are. Jesus is there the entire time, though, calling our name and waiting for us to move towards Him because He wants to show us how He can take something that is broken and turn it into something that is beautiful. That He can still fulfill even if we fail.

I imagine Jesus, knowing what we are going through, just sitting and waiting for us to speak up on things that we've tried to hold in or get control of for so long, saying, "Why didn't you just tell me?" That Jesus would much rather take our pains and start working rather than see us hurting. Because Jesus is about getting us to a place of victory, but from us, it will take vulnerability. He isn't seeking out to save who we pretend to be but our most authentic self— failures, falls, and all. If we can be honest with God, we will know we are being honest with ourselves. In order to have victory, we must be vulnerable with our valleys.

As we walk through this journey toward vulnerability, my hope is that this book inspires you to know that you can be both vulnerable and victorious. I would say it's hard to be victorious without being vulnerable. Often times when we pick up a book, our hope is that we can see opportunities where we can change and become better in whatever it is that we are reading about, but change often comes through a challenge.

Some of us read business books because we want to be better in our business, or we read about cooking because we want to make something better than what we toss in the microwave. No matter what you are reading up on or learning about, there's one thing that stands out in all of it. Doing is the difference between staying the same and being better. My hope is that what you read becomes an opportunity to become an act of expression. And that even the small steps you may take are incredibly significant.

This journey may find you seeing hurts from the past that have been covered up begin to come up to the surface again and stretch you to deal with them. You may find that you'll have some decisions to make with the current friend-ships you have, what you will need to choose to finally be vulnerable about, or maybe just how you see yourself. But that even in the midst of all of that, you would simply come. You'll find more relief in honesty than in hiding. Some of the consequences we have chosen for ourselves by hiding have made for more painful consequences than if we just chose to be vulnerable. My hope for you is that as we begin to speak up, we'll begin to see something new.

If I am honest with everyone and anyone reading this, I have to say that I don't even feel fully qualified to write a book like this. I am still working through being vulnerable about some of the doubts, fears, worries, and anxieties that I have dealt with in my own life. My encouragement to you is that the thief may have managed for a moment or two, mak-ing you feel the pain of what's taken from you, but this is the day to take back what's been stolen. That when the serpent manages to get crafty, that you can still run to the craftsman. That there is enough grace that can be given, even to the greatest fall you have ever experienced. That even though you feel like you are dying, you can come back to life, and even though you have faced some setbacks, there can also be come-backs.

I believe that as you page through these chapters, you'll find that your trust in God grows to the place where you can release what you have tried to keep hidden and give Him what you have by choosing vulnerability. That you can find a voice, know the purpose, and live in the victory that comes with choosing vulnerability to experience growing faith, deeper friendships, greater freedom, and a brighter future. And at the end of the day, I would guess to say that those are the things that are the most important to you and what you spend the most amount of time on because they are what you most want to be successful in and are what you look to when you think of a full life.

It wasn't easy, but in the end, I managed to come clean to "carpetgate" in a moment with my mom. We look back on it now and laugh about how ugly that white carpet managed to look with just that one juice stain on it, but after many rounds of steaming it, the stain was gone, and I was set free. But the real freedom I experienced was the moment I became vulnerable and recognized that there was more relationship and forgiveness than any amount of Kool-Aid that could have ever ended up on that carpet. God is ready to bring you forgiveness, healing, and relationship.

All you need to do is come.

CHAPTER TWO

THE VOICE OF VULNERABILITY
LIFE BEHIND THE SCENES

I love documentaries. I probably have an unhealthy obsession with them. My wife gets frustrated because any time we are on the couch in front of the TV, she wants to watch a movie, and I want to watch how a movie is made. She usually wins, so I go make some popcorn, sit down, and we carry on happily. I get it. Documentaries aren't for everyone.

I love documentaries because they give you the truth. They give you the full, uncut, no-details-left-behind story. The movie is the final, finished, and perfect product that the producers want you to see. The one where every line is perfectly placed with emphasis and drama. The hero manages to slide through the small open crack at the exact moment before the collapsing wall crashes down, leaving them in a puddle of pain. Or the championship-winning catch with zero seconds left on the clock leading to a team hugging and celebrating in perfect harmony. I'm all for being excited to see victory at the end of a movie or a sports season, but tell me the reality of what it really took for you to lift up the Lombardi trophy or the Oscar for best movie. Pull back the curtain and take me behind the scenes so I can see the realness of what you went through to put together the ideal that is displayed.

Maybe you like movies like my wife because, in the end, we all want to feel like the hero with what we do, whether that be an inspirational writer, a good husband or wife, having a successful career, or just someone who can be a true version of themselves. The truth is, though, that when we go behind the scenes of our lives, oftentimes, what we discover is the opposite of what it is we wish to see. It's one thing to see the behind-the-scenes of someone else, but when we are being documented, it feels like an entirely different story. My love for documentaries and uncovering the reality behind the ideal and all the work that we see has left me with a question to wrestle with.

How do we be vulnerable about what we go through?

It's easy for us to highlight our highlights and share all of our successes—to release and promote the finely edited, well-scripted, cinematic version of our lives. I'm convinced, though, that Jesus wants something different. Jesus took us behind the scenes and reminded us that humanity would have difficulty. We would have moments where we would miss a cue or forget a line. Jesus spent a lot of time talking about what it would look like for us to know what victory is, and it always involved coming to Him and sharing with Him. It's easy to want to think that it should take so much more than that or that Jesus wants you to give the performance of your life or to figure out how to do the most good in order for you to get to Him, but it's not. Jesus isn't looking for the edited version you give, but the unedited version that you actually live.

OUT OF HIDING

Remember the game hide-and-seek? You probably played it at some point as a kid, and the only reason you might still be playing it today is that you have kids. Any other reason would just be weird or criminal. But we tend to do this with our lives. We become pros at hiding what is hard. We work to convince everyone on the outside that everything is gold trophies because their response to believing how happy we are and how good we are doing at living is what will make us feel like we have victory. It's easy to become convinced that life is exactly like the way we are portraying it. What I've realized in my own life, though, is that not choosing to live vulnerably was actually robbing me of victory.

Jesus' idea of victory for us is not how we think about ourselves but knowing Him and how He sees us. People who know how Jesus sees them understand that they can share the very things that are breaking and burdening them and know that He won't scold them but can save and strengthen them. People who know the truth of how Jesus sees them are able to live with the weight lifted off of their shoulders and live in the lightness of freedom. He wants us to live in the victory that cost Him a steep price.

It's not always easy to be moved to truth when you've managed to remain comfortable in staying hidden for so long. The truth can sometimes be a painful thing to endure. The reason why truth is so painful is probably because it can remind us of how lost we really are. Discovering the truth takes us to the place of what is really taking place in our lives. If the truth was so easy, we would probably just blurt it out like we are playing a game of Pictionary. We can get lost in the ebbs and flows of life's experiences and wonder how we got here. We look around and wonder which way gets us back to the place of victory.

Have you ever gotten lost before? My mom always tells this story about the time that I got lost in a JC Penny department store. This was at the time when they still were able to order from those insanely huge catalogs that they shipped to your house. They had every type of color and curtain fabric in them. There was nothing that was pennies at JC Penny.

While my parents stood at the ordering counter, being inspired by the idea of what would look best in our living room, I had my sights set on stickers. You know you'd made it as a department store when you have an aisle completely dedicated to stickers. I casually walked away to where I wanted to because that's what four-year-olds who don't know any better do. I managed to find the aisle of stickers. I was in Heaven. I pulled sticker sleeves off the shelves and was in awe of all the shapes, colors, and characters. I may have even opened up a few of them and did an adhesive test to make sure they would stick. I wasn't a criminal. I was a four-year-old. My parents were so panicked when they realized that I was lost that the perfect drapes for our living room windows did not matter much anymore.

STICK OR STUCK?

In our search to discover truth and life, it can quickly turn into us searching for what we think will stick. All the while, we walk away from what it is that provides us with full security and satisfaction. We get lost in relationships or sleepless nights trying to climb the corporate ladder. We get lost in a substitution for the truth, hoping it will lead to life when all it leads to is feeling like we've been lied to. The lie makes us wonder what we believe anymore and leaves us stuck figuring out where we go from here.

So what now? How do we get unstuck? How do we find our way back? Jesus is the greatest guide when it comes to those who are feeling lost. That is actually the reason why He came. His mission was and still is guiding the lost. He is in the business of retrieving those who are having a hard time believing and does it with grace and truth. The voice of vulnerability that leads to victory speaks honestly. Jesus even had to help the disciples, his closest learners, with their feeling of deception and disbelief. It starts with Jesus washing the disciples' feet and predicting a betrayal and a denial over dinner. Talk about an awkward dinner. Check, please. I'm sure, for the disciples, this had to be a hard truth to swallow. They gave up their lives to follow Jesus. They spent time growing and knowing Jesus that nobody in their right mind would ever do something like this. I'm sure it led to some of them considering if they had made the right decision. They felt lost and at a loss.

One of the greatest qualities of a guide is their ability to be understanding. They know what it is that you're going through, and they can discern what you yearn. One of my favorite days of school was always the first day. And not just because I got to bust open a fresh box of Crayola markers or see my friends or the girl that made me excited about going back to school. The reason I loved the first day was that it was syllabus day. Now, I mainly loved it because I knew I wasn't getting homework, so it felt like a bonus day before the tragedy of homework would strike. I remember looking at the outline, seeing the game plan of the assignments for the semester, and turning the page like I was cranking the lever of a jack in the box to see what the final project was. If you had a good teacher, though, the final paper or project may have had you panicked, but the comfort of time and the communication of your teacher gave you relief with what you saw and felt. Find someone who will stick with you when you get stuck.

UNTROUBLED

Seven words remind me that Jesus is both comforting and understanding in the midst of the truth that we are receiving:

"Do not let your hearts be troubled" John 14:1

These are the seven words that are said to the disciples after their awkward dinner reveal, and I believe that they are the same words that He would say to you. He says these words because He knows that what is troubling our hearts hinders us from trusting with our hearts.

The voice of vulnerability speaks through trusting in the midst of what is troubling. And trusting in the right person leads to peace. Jesus is actually preparing a place of peace at this very moment. He is putting together a future for you, and all it takes from you is trust. I'm sure if you watched anybody do something crazy before, then you probably have heard the word faith. Faith and trust go hand in hand. They are one and the same. Faith is the currency of eternity. And Jesus wants us to be there with Him. He wants us to be there so much that He's going to make a return trip to Earth and take us to be with Him. A good guide doesn't just give you a plan; they go to you and take you with them. The path to this person and place comes through faith.

Trust and faith can be difficult sometimes because it is taking something out of your hands and placing it into someone else's. Trust is a choice and a response. Jesus said to not let your hearts be troubled. He didn't say I prohibit your hearts from being troubled. He offered us the opportunity to experience victory. Whatever you are choosing is what you are allowing. And what you are allowing often becomes your reaction or response.

Worry is the enemy of trusting. Worry is our reaction

to take back everything that was already handed over, believing we can manufacture something faster and better. Our worrying can lead us to do things that become more troubling. I have a little bit of a stubborn streak in me, along with perfectionism, so I can have a difficult time letting things go. It mostly lands in the category of projects I am working on. I worry that it won't look how I want it to or that I won't finish on time. Or that someone will look at all the effort I put into something and not see it with the same value that I see it. I'm starting to realize that things work out much better when I choose to be a learner instead of a worrier.

DOUBT HUMBLED OUT

I think we tend to give Thomas, one of the disciples of Jesus that we've nicknamed the "doubting disciple," a half unfair assessment. I'm sure if he was here today and knew we called him a doubter, he would tweet or post a Facebook status and have something to say about it. I'm sure it would look something like:

"You would want proof, too, if someone you saw get crucified managed to resurrect from the dead and then showed up in your living room." #notalone

We famously know him as a doubter, and Jesus did tell him not to doubt over the show and tell of His scars. I like to think of Thomas as a guy who was also genuinely trying to be a learner. I mean, how many friends do you still have in your life that constantly doubt everything? I don't know how long you would still be friends. I don't know how long Thomas would have lasted as a disciple if he spent all of his time doubting every single thing that went on. The word disciple in the Greek language actually translates to "learner." And I can relate with him in that I am a visual learner, too. So, when Thomas asked Jesus how to know the way to where He was going, Thomas started by calling Him "Lord." Doubting without humility is what keeps you from learning. Jesus didn't question his intelligence or roast him in front of all the other disciples. He just said, "You're looking at Him." Okay, Jesus didn't say it quite like that, but pretty close. Jesus actually said this:

"I am the way and the truth and the life."

I love the way this is set up because when I read it I can't help but read it as:

I am the way that brings you the truth that leads to the life. You want freedom? You want peace? You want life? It's coming through me.

The way that we approach truth leads to the life that we have. The life of freedom is found in the sound of humility. The voice of vulnerability that leads to victory sounds like humility.

It's easy for us to switch the "I am" to being about us and what we can do. That seems way too risky and overwhelming to try to take matters into your own hands for a little bit of pride and reputation. The lie wants to boost your pride. To tell you that you can live a certain way behind the scenes, and no one will ever know. That you can find your own way and prove everyone wrong. That you have enough power to get unstuck. Jesus was very pointed when it came to pride. He knew how pride has the ability of leaving a person destined to end up deceived and alone. That pride has a way of keeping us from knowing and being loved. Pride has a way of making us try and look better now, but making us feel worse later. We become greedy for personal progress instead of growing through the process.

Jesus just wants you to lay down the lie and the pride and come to Him. Because if you don't lay it down, it could end up being your hang-up. I think it's what Judas wished he knew. Judas wasn't just some random hitman that showed up the week of Jesus' arrest and death. This was the one who had followed Jesus around. Not only did Jesus invite Judas to dinner despite Judas being the enemy at the table, but He also prayed for Judas in the garden just before the guards showed up. The guards got their man, and Judas got his money. Judas recognized what he'd done, but instead of embracing the radical grace of Jesus, he was stuck with shame. If only Judas knew that if he would have come to Jesus with all that was inside of him, he wouldn't have been called the betrayer. He would have been called a brother. When you are vulnerable with Jesus, He doesn't call you by what you do or who you are, but whose you are.

The path of the lie always leads to a dead-end. Ever ended up at a dead end? Usually, it has some type of cement block or barricades that sits there like a road construction casket. People toss their empty Hostess wrappers and cans of Dr. Pepper there because they figure no one wants to be there anyway. The worst part about a dead-end is you can't go forward or see anything beyond. Boring. It's time to trade the litter for living and our dead ends for our destiny. It's time to get back on the path that was carved out for us two thousand years ago that leads to purpose and power.

He came for you so that you would come to Him. But in order for us to turn around, we need to know and be vulnerable about coming to the end of where we thought we could take ourselves, and instead take the hand of the guide into victorious living.

Just before you hit a dead-end, there's always a sign that warns you about the dead-end coming up. God is so gracious that He even will give us signs that warn us that we are approaching a dead-end. Look for the sign. It can be a painful feeling when you see the sign and realize what would have been the best choice all along. But it is at that moment when you choose to humble yourself that you begin to learn about yourself. You remember all the turns you took and which turns would have been right. The broken pieces that you tried to take and humbly put them back into the hands of the one who knows best. And when you put the pieces back into God's hands, He's not shaming you. He's celebrating you.

GOLD STICKERS

I was eventually found that day in the sticker aisle of JC Penny. I don't know how long I was lost because to a four-year-old in a sticker aisle, minutes away felt like seconds for me. I'm sure for my parents, though, seconds felt like hours as they frantically searched up and down aisles and under clothing racks trying to find me. I'm pretty sure my name might have even been called over the employee intercom. When they found me, I was standing exactly in the spot I was when they started frantically searching for me. I didn't understand all of what was going on, but I could tell that when they found me, they celebrated. So much to the point where they bought me a pack of stickers.

Going through life, I've had many moments where I felt like I was lost. Sometimes I still do. It wasn't in the sticker aisle of a JC Penny, but the feeling of being stuck still exists. Jesus doesn't panic when we feel lost. He knows the behind the scenes of our lives, and if we are willing to speak with honestly, in a tone that is trusting, with the sound of humility, we'll find ourselves found. He knew where we were all along and was preparing to come and get us. And when He does, He isn't criticizing our past or questioning our present but celebrating and bringing clarity to our future. He slaps a gold sticker on you and shows you the way to life and light. The voice of vulnerability is speaking honestly in humility because you choose to be someone who is trusting. You can be vulnerable because He is available and sustainable. When you're looking for the way to be vulnerable and victorious, He'll point you back to the documentary and remind you:

You're looking at Him.

CHAPTER THREE

RECIPE FOR CLARITY
SHOWING UP TO DINNER

Everybody has someone and something they are passionate about. My passion is people. I love people. Being a pastor, most of my days are spent around people. I enjoy searching the world and find satisfaction in sharing life with people and hearing the pages of the story that is their lives. I'm usually the guy that you are angry at because he holds up the line at the grocery store. If you ever see me around, I recommend that you turn around and find a new line or go through self-checkout.

My other passion lately has been trying new foods. I love searching around to try the latest mash-up of two ingredients that no one previously thought of. I'm convinced I could make a career of it if I wanted to. I'm still waiting for the Food Network to call me back. There's just something about peeling back the wrapper and feeling like you have uncovered a national treasure. My last search left me with a piece of deep-fried chicken sandwiched in between two glazed donuts. It was like I was on a date with diabetes. I still ate the whole thing.

As I've gone along this passion of discovering and eating new foods, I've also discovered something new that I am equally not passionate about: cooking. I can't cook. I make an oven nervous. It doesn't sweat because of the heat. It sweats because of people like me. I probably shouldn't even be allowed to own one. One Thanksgiving, we were putting together a dinner for a bunch of middle and high schoolers. And by we, I mean an army of parents who actually knew how to operate a kitchen. I was handed a frozen pie to toss in the oven. All I had to do was slide the pumpkin pie in the oven. Before I knew it, that poor pumpkin pie was dripping delicious debris all over the oven. Why? Thinking it was a potential fire hazard, I took the pie out of the pie tin before I put it in the oven.

Nailed it.

There's nothing better to me than mixing the someone and the something that I love. Trying new food is fun and re-freshing, but it tastes so much better when you have someone to share the experience with. I am definitely a "Yes, please," person when it comes to sitting over a table full of food and getting lost in conversations about life. Food can do wonders when it comes to comforting us to open up about real life.

My lack of passion for cooking has left me with a problem when it comes to my passion for people. I love talking so much that I even talk out the recipe as I'm making it, and it still doesn't turn out. I'm convinced sharing anything I'm making won't be enjoyable. It might not even be edible. The last thing I want to see is someone I know watching their eyes water in pain as they are trying to compliment me while choking down the dinner I made. My wife and I breathe a sigh of relief when someone asks us to come over to their house for dinner because we know that means we will probably stay friends.

TASTE TEST

I don't always get the recipe right when it comes to following Jesus, but I like to think I am getting something right when I realize He also loved people and food. If you look through scripture, you'll notice that Jesus was known for His love and many miracles, but also for His dinner parties. David even used a verse in Psalm 34 that reminds us of food and just how good Jesus is.

"Taste and see that the Lord is good."

Everything Jesus puts together ends up tasting good. It's hard sometimes for us to say the same for our own lives. For some reason, when it comes to this journey of life and faith that we are on, we short, confuse, forget, and substitute ourselves of what will give us victory. We got bitter and substituted the sugar for salt. We shorted ourselves of courage and confidence and lived below the level of our potential. We stayed in one spot for too long and managed to get burnt. No matter which one happens, we usually end up feeling disappointed with the results. Vulnerability can feel a lot like bringing a bad dish to a dinner party.

What happens when it's time to put what we made on the table? How do we share what even we ourselves really don't care for? What happens when it's time to peel back the tin foil and share when you don't like what life has made?

The best and the hardest part for us is that Jesus doesn't want you to just throw it away. He doesn't expect you to eat it either. And He definitely doesn't want you to bring something you ordered from somewhere else and claim it as yours. He wants you to show up, share, and step out. Are you ready?

THREE INGREDIENTS

Matthew 7:7 gives us a great, not-so-secret recipe for getting real. And the best part is that it isn't a bunch of complex ingredients that involve math to figure out, and it guarantees results. It says:

"Ask, and it will be given to you; seek, and you will find; knock, and the door will be opened to you."

Just like any good dinner party, vulnerability involves these three ingredients. Thinking it through. Talking it out. Taking it home.

I'll bet when you set up dinner plans with friends, there is always one question that works its way into the conversation. It's the same one that Jesus likes to ask us when we can't see a life beyond the one we have.

What do you want?

Jesus specifically liked to ask blind people this question. It wasn't because He had temporary amnesia or wanted to clarify with them just to make sure. He wanted to hear it from them. And He wants to hear it from you. For the blind guys in scripture, it was a no brainer. They spent most of their lives thinking about the day that they would be able to see.

For some people, the question is as clear as day. You make those thoughts your full-time job. I don't want to feel alone. I don't want my failures hanging over my head. I want to finally just say what it is that I've been holding in. But knowing what you want doesn't always feel in plain sight. Saying what you want for dinner is easy. Saying what you want for your life seems harder. We fumble around through the question because we didn't really give it much thought. Or maybe we are just surprised that someone has taken an interest in us. Jesus takes interest in you.

Take some time to think about what you want if you haven't yet. I find that when I really want something, if I stop and pay attention to what I want, I will discover why I want it. It's easy for us to share without having thought about any real direction. Ask social media.

Imagine if everything that was shared without thought was like driving a car. I hope that person has good insurance because chances are they would be swerving all over the place. There is power in pausing. We're told that when we decide to be still, we will know God. Think about what you want and think about what God wants. And then be vulnerable and be prepared to ask for it. Jesus gives you permission to. And when you do, you won't be left on your own to starve.

Sometimes you'll find that what you thought you wanted and what Jesus gives you aren't the same thing. That's only because Jesus is good enough to give you what you need. And you'll be healthier in the long run for it. Getting what you need isn't always easy initially. I like pizza. I eat it a lot. It's what I want. My wife opts for vegetables. It's probably what I need. Sometimes I feel like it's going to kill me. Until I realize it's because she loves me and wants me to live a long life.

Jesus is the same way. He wants you to have victory and clarity. And whatever that looks like, He is prepared to do it. It's what gives us the faith and confidence to ask in the first place. He gave His life for it and dedicates Himself to it. You're the number one guest on His list.

TAKE IT TO THE TABLE

I love food, but I love what happens around food even more. You know you're at a good dinner when you leave having learned something about yourself and someone else. If you've ever been to one that isn't like that, I'll bet whoever was with you was texting you and elbowing you under the table to wrap it up and get out of there. It's incredible what you find out as you begin to talk it out. I think that's what Jesus meant when He said, "Seek, and you will find." He meant to simply talk it out with Him. Take it to the table.

I've found it difficult sometimes to find the right words to say with some of the people I have had the pleasure of sitting across from. They don't mean to do it, but it's easy to get caught up in how superior they seem in comparison to us. The kitchen is clean. Fancy decoration on the walls. Everything is placed in exactly the right spot. We can start to feel pretty small and feel like we weren't worthy for a seat at the table. Instead of talking it out, we start to talk it up. It's easy to compare when we feel like no one will care about what we share. When that thought tries to ruin you and change your response, remember that Jesus invited you to be the real you. Jesus wants real hearts, not just right words. He is looking at His prize, and it's you.

The best way to seek is to start. Don't know what to say? Start with a question. Good seeking usually does. You'll find out that what matters to you matters to Him. You don't need to come up with Harvard-level words. This isn't a press release; this is a diary. It's not meant to be about strategy as much as it is about sharing. Jesus is coming not for a lecture but for a conversation. You are coming to Jesus with your dish and wondering how to make it better.

Give God all your questions, including the ones about your pains, setbacks, and feelings. Share where you're at. Ask Him why things are happening. Ask why you feel the way you do. Ask how to work through it. You may not feel like you have all the words to say, and that's okay. He's the chef and understands the recipe.

You may feel embarrassed or ashamed because of all the measurements that didn't manage to measure up. You may feel like He is going to taste what you have to say and go all Gordon Ramsey on you. You'll find Jesus to be a friend. When you come to Him, He isn't looking to critique but to show compassion.

Sharing about yourself in the most honest way is caring for yourself in the greatest way. Mom always said, "Sharing is caring." And sometimes, we don't know that until we just follow through. When we bring our worst to Him, He gives us His very best. Sharing vulnerably is sharing the pain of who you think you are in exchange for the potential of who God sees you becoming. To show us our value as we are being vulnerable. Trading our recipe that led to disaster for a recipe that will lead to destiny. And for Jesus, that's what us being at the table was all about in the first place.

TAKE IT TO GO

At some point, it is time to get up from the table and go. My wife and I love people, so that also makes us bad at saying goodbye and getting out the door. When you hang out with us, you're guaranteed a goodbye, followed by a side conversation, and then another goodbye. This happens probably at least two more times. We know as much as we enjoyed sharing the highs and lows through laughter and tears, we can't stay at the table forever. That would just be weird. At some point, it's time to get up from the table and take a step.

When we've put everything out on the table, we'll start to see where we are headed. It's easy for us to sometimes decide that we are just going to linger around at the table, when Jesus wants us to go out and live. He doesn't just want to share with you, but show you that what He is sharing works. He gave us permission not just to only ask Him but to join Him. I'll take that offer. One of Jesus' favorite phrases was "follow me." He said it to two brothers who sat in a boat looking until they decided to lay down their nets. Following is agreeing to what is being shared. Whatever Jesus has spoken into us now is what He wants to be lived out through us next. Jesus is about your bright future. In order to head in that direction, you need to go.

"Go" is one of the other phrases that Jesus liked to use most when he was talking with his friends. Those people he spoke to are ordinary people like you and me with pains and problems. Our problems and pains of the past often hold us back from going in the present. We can start to think that our past will haunt and reject us from having the victorious life we want to live. It can pull us into doubt and make us question if we are sure that what we heard will work. But Jesus isn't concerned about the past because he cares about the present that leads to the future. He cares so much about our going that he turned it from a verb into a command. He wants you to move in the present towards that greater future. That's why we share at the table, so that we can take the next step.

Taking a step to share is rarely easy right away. Sometimes it even manages to feel risky and crazy. It may even want to convince you to stay put. I think the only risky and crazy thing is not having vulnerability and victory.

Remember when you were a baby? Okay, that's a dumb question. I don't think anyone does. But at some point, I'm sure you've watched a video that your parents recorded of you taking your first steps. They probably were making weird noises and doing some high-pitched business negotiating so that you would start walking. You may have gotten to see your first steps, but you probably didn't see the countless amount of times the camera was out when you tried to take a step and fell flat on your face. All that footage got recorded over with birthday parties and bath times.

It took a lot of attempts for you to get your footing, but, at some point, you learned to walk. Now you don't even need to think twice about the steps you're taking. Being vulnerable can feel the same way. You'll fall flat on your face sometimes. It could leave you with a bruise. Bruises heal. Just remember that Jesus is keeping every great moment where you take a step and will play it back for you in some way, someday. He isn't playing the tape of your failures but the tape of your victories. Each step that you take to share will make you stronger. These steps, as they knock you on the ground, will open up the door to new places and new opportunities.

   If there's anything I could hope for you in this chapter, it would be that you choose to share and embrace the new. Don't look for it to happen by chance, but ask, seek and knock by choice. Jesus didn't ask us to bump into Him. He asked us to follow and go. And the best part is that you are not alone. I love when our friends care package what's left of dinner for us before we leave. It's like bonus lunch for the next day. Every time I take out what's left over from dinner, I'm reminded what we ate, but even more what we shared. God does the same thing. It's not packaged in the form of food, but packaged in the form of His spirit. His spirit reminds you of what you shared and how He cares. God isn't absent or uncaring when it comes to the time when you need to share. Remember, His greatest promises weren't just about His ability but about His availability.

"And surely I am with you always to the very end of the age."

CHAPTER FOUR

THAT ONE THING
GETTING OFF THE COUCH

One of my wife's favorite superhero movies is Guardians of the Galaxy. We actually have one of the Guardians living in our house. Shortly after we got married, we decided it was time to take the next step in our marriage. We got a dog. I drove hours to a middle-of-nowhere farm that I was convinced got hit with a plague of mosquitos. There, I picked up our new nine-week-old pug and brought him home as a surprise for my wife. She fell in love all over again and gave our dog the name Groot.

I enjoy surprising my wife, and the dog enjoys surprising me. Especially on the living room floor. He should work for UPS. He's great at deliveries. Not a huge fan of that. Regardless, I love our dog. He makes me feel more like an adult, and he's buying me a little time before my wife starts talking about the kids we'll have that we won't name after Guardians of the Galaxy characters. Even if I think Rocket would make for a pretty sweet kid's name. This dog is also helping me learn about myself. He's laying on my shoulder inspiring me as I'm writing this.

At the house, Groot manages to get away with quite a bit. I don't know if it's the smashed in face or the fact that he's the first living thing we've had the responsibility of taking care of, but he's got a pretty long leash. Somewhere between my wife consistently giving him carrots and frozen blueberries to now hogging up our bed space at night, he tested his freedom on the one thing we are the most dictatorial about.

There is a couch in our sunroom. There isn't really anything special about this blue couch beside the fact that it is owned by my sister and her husband. We have another sectional couch that sits in the living room that is about twenty feet away from this blue couch. We never yell at Groot for being on our long comfortable sectional. I think we've actually encouraged it at points. But it doesn't matter. He has set his sights on the blue couch. He knows he isn't supposed to be on it, so he looks around like a secret agent to see if anyone is looking before he makes his move. He has even tried to remind us that it is his couch with his special marking. I can't tell you how many times I've come close to losing my voice. Sometimes I think I am a parrot with how many times I tell him to get off the couch. Sometimes we just stop trying while he perches on the couch barking at the old lady walking her dog down our street. She probably thinks we own a monster.

Most of us have what I will for the rest of this chapter call "our one thing." It is the thing that we don't want to be attached to but also manage to go back to. It is what we are most wanting to vulnerably share about. The one thing that seems to continually take us back to the couch. We know it isn't where we are supposed to be. Even when we say it's the last time on the couch or we hear something that reminds us that we aren't supposed to be there, we somehow still manage to find our way back.

One of the things that my dog loves most about that couch is that it gives him access to see out the windows. Sometimes, he manages to see his reflection and begins to bark at himself. It's comical because it's him. It's not as comical when it comes to us.

We go where we aren't supposed to go hoping to see something more than what we typically see. We may see something, but ultimately, we end up seeing our reflection in the mirror, yelling at ourselves about how we got here. For you, maybe it's been a relationship with someone or something that posed itself as life-giving, and you realize now it's life-taking. Maybe it's a decision you crawl back to because it's something that sits in your family history. Maybe it's something that makes you forget the feelings of rejection and insecurity but then comes and amplifies the very things you were trying to forget. It leaves you wondering if there is a life beyond your one thing. I'm sure if you've ever dealt with that one thing, you've asked yourself some questions.

How do I not be consumed by this one thing?
What will it take to get victory over it?
Will I ever be able to step away from this?
How do I start doing the things I want to do?

DENIAL DONE

There's a verse that Paul wrote that sums up how we feel when it comes to that one thing. To many, it's probably considered the ultimate tongue twister of scripture. In Romans 7, Paul says:

> "I do not understand what I do. For what I want to do I do not do, but what I hate I do." Romans 7:15

Try to say that ten times fast. Trying to understand why we do what we do feels as difficult as trying to say that. It's probably one of the reasons why you picked up this book. You don't understand what you do, but now you want to be vulnerable, walk through the valley, and have victory. You don't want to continually be stuck in what you don't want to do, but you want to get caught up in the things that you are supposed to do. You want to do good; for yourself and the people around you. You want your one thing to be the right thing. Nobody really ever wakes up and says, "I think today is the day that I think I'll start doing that thing I don't want to do."

Big things usually don't happen immediately. It's many small decisions along the way that turned that small thing into a big thing. And now the big thing seems large and in charge over the things that we know we are supposed to do. Before we know it, the direction that we once had starts to feel like distance and separation. That separation can start to make us feel like we are losing our voice and hearing the voice that wants to lead us. Fortunately for us, Jesus hasn't lost his voice in any of it. He patiently works in every shape and size, no matter how big or small it seems to us. Just ask Peter.

Peter was all about doing the right thing. He was a trophy disciple. He had his moments of stubbornness, just like all of us do, but he was loyal. He was one of Jesus's closest followers. You can imagine how dumbfounded and devastated Peter was when he was told by Jesus that he would deny Jesus. And not just one time, but three times. For Peter, his one thing would be denying. The man who was ready to take on death and prison for Jesus, was now taking oaths that he never knew him. It's a far jump, but it's often how we feel when that one thing manages to work its way in.

I don't have the greatest memory. I can be really good at remembering things that don't really matter, like movie quotes. I'm really bad at remembering things that do matter, like my wallet. Before we go anywhere, my wife is constantly reminding me to check if I have my wallet. Then I remind her to check if she has her phone. It's a rough day when I call her to ask where my wallet is. Somehow, we manage.

Reminders are often the warning now that has the potential of keeping us from worrying later. My wife reminds me about my wallet because she cares. It's a rough and embarrassing moment when you reach for your wallet only to realize that it isn't there. Restaurants and police officers aren't a fan of it. The reminding keeps the consequence that could have come from what you didn't do from happening. When Jesus gives the warning to Peter and when He gives it to you, it's so that you would remember. The reminding is for remembering, and it's all done out of caring.

As much as we are reminded and try to remember, sometimes our one thing still manages to make us forget our relationship with Jesus and the right thing. The heat of the moment can feel like it brings us warmth now but makes us feel burned later. Peter's denials were even found around fires. Not only did Peter deny being a disciple, but he even forgot the name of the man he loyally followed. When we follow our one thing, we quickly can forget who we are and who God is. We can get consumed in how our one thing serves us. We abandon all that we know for the sake of satisfying ourselves. We cash in the things that hold high value for the ones that don't.

Our humanity can make us act selfishly. Our one thing becomes the first thing, but not the right thing, so it becomes the destructive thing. We can lose sight of what was just seen and begin to live in survival mode. God doesn't want you to get caught up in living a life that is set up to merely survive. He wants you to thrive and to serve. We all get sidetracked from time to time. We get in moments where we trade in our trophies for ribbons. For Peter, he would recognize what he had done through the reminder of a rooster. For us, our reminder comes through God's spirit. The sound may be different, but the message is the same. Your one thing does not need to be your ending. Redemption is coming.

BACK TO THE MAIN THING

Hopeless and helpless are two words that can accurately describe someone who has just been hit by their one thing. Maybe you've felt that. Our one thing can make us feel like we are lacking in our present and losing our future. Maybe you've been stuck in your one thing for a long time. You wish you would have been able to figure it out after the third time. Just when we begin to think that there is no chance for a second chance, Jesus rises up to redeem and reinstate us. How do I know this? He did the same for Peter. Literally. He resurrects from the dead. And He isn't resurrecting to remind you of what you've done. He's coming to remind you of who you are. He isn't coming to indict you. He's coming to inspire you. He wants to take you back to your yes.

I remember the way the room looked, where I was sitting, who I was sitting next to, and who I planned to talk to after it was done. Sitting in the back row of a youth service held in the downstairs gym of a church, my polo-wearing, freshman-looking self made the decision to say yes. It wasn't the first time I had said yes. I had made that decision before in the exact same room. I was back where I started because, along the way, I had let some things get in the way that took me to the same places I had been before I said yes. Until a rooster-crow-moment for me helped me recognize the voice, again, that was calling out to me. The voice left me with a choice. Do I continue to stay where I was, or do I move forward to where I wanted to be? It was time to do something different than the same thing I had been doing. It took me going back to where it began to respond again.

God has a way of taking us back to where it began to get our attention. For Peter, it took him back to the Sea of Galilee. The place where he abandoned his career as a fisherman for the sake of becoming a follower. Our one thing has a way of calling us to return back to what we find familiar. We let our feelings of missing the mark make us feel like we are only worthy of a mundane life. We sell ourselves short of the great mission waiting for us. We can't see beyond what is in front of us, so we return back to the life we lived before we became a follower.

Jesus still stands on the shore and calls out to us. Peter didn't even notice Jesus from the boat until he heard Jesus remind him of the moment that Peter met him for the first time. And when he finally recognizes, there's no time to remember how he sank because he's too busy swimming.

You can swim too. When we are on the boat feeling like we are watching the life we want to live drift away, Jesus is calling out to us, reminding us of where we want to be so that we can respond. Your one thing will try to yell out to not respond, to remind you of how much weight is on you, that you will somehow fail at coming to Jesus too. Have a plan because having victory over our one thing is going to require multiple levels of response. Jesus is just looking for one response, and that is to start swimming.

If you can't swim, then float. Jesus is patient enough to wait for you. Make your way towards him. Responding is the difference between staying and living. That one thing that left you feeling like you were sinking is not what Jesus is thinking. Jesus can't change who you pretend to be. He wants you to bring yourself first. And when you meet Jesus on the shore where you want to be, he's not looking to empty you but to fill you, not to berate you. He's looking to celebrate over breakfast with you.

You're able to have a fresh start because Jesus is in the business of giving people a fresh start. For that to happen, it is all about us giving what we have and receiving what he gives. Trust me, it's not a fair trade, and we get the better end of that deal. It's like when you trade your younger brother four pennies for a dollar because he thinks four is more than one. Jesus knows what he's getting in the deal, and he's happy to do it because it includes you.

The hardest part when it comes to our one thing is letting go. We've hung onto it for so long. We know it has no value, but we can't part with it because we've tried to give it value. It makes us feel a certain way. Comforting us, but also killing us. Jesus understands that. He didn't say this life would be easy, but he did say he would be here. He gives four words to Peter and to us to make handing it over easier. He says:

"Do you love me?"

Jesus was always good at asking questions. These four words can feel insulting when you've spent the better part of your life sacrificing and following. Peter just jumped out of a boat and got soaking wet. Does Jesus need reminding I love him? No. Jesus wasn't asking the question for his sake; he was asking for yours. Jesus knew that. The question wasn't asked to know if Jesus was loved. Someone who is all-knowing already knew that. The question was asked to be loving. Jesus doesn't need to be built up. He's Jesus. We are not. And that means that sometimes we need to be built up. Jesus multiplies the question by three so that Peter walks away remembering love and not his one thing.

You're reinstated by simply receiving the love Jesus gives. He looks you in the eye and asks you if you love him. Not because he is needing, but so that you know he can be trusted. He asks you the question so that as you speak vulnerably, you can live confidently. He loves you enough to ask the question because He wants you to be led to a life that experiences victory. Your one thing wants you to return to your vomit like a dog. It's gross, but it's in Proverbs. Go look it up. Jesus wants you to come back to victory. And it comes through receiving his restoring. It isn't done through logic or lectures. It's done through love.

FROM COUCH TO COURAGE

Some of you might be asking yourselves another question.

How do I know when I've found victory over that one thing?

At the beginning of this chapter, I mentioned that our

one thing is often put together and persuaded through our ability to be selfish. The way we know that our one thing is destroyed and disposed of is through the choice to be self-less. You'll know you are receiving love given to you when you respond by giving it to others. Peter knew exactly what Jesus meant when he said to take care of his sheep. The same love that you received is the same love that you now get the opportunity to lead in. For Peter, that love led to one of the greatest and most powerful messages he ever shared. The same can happen to you. Your vulnerability can take your one thing and turn it into something that could mean everything to somebody.

To put it simply, get off the couch. I find that the longer I sit, the greater chance I have to fall asleep and the more my bones ache when I get up. You may have been sitting for a while. It may hurt to stand. It may take a few attempts. Everything in you may not want to. That's okay. God is patient and understanding. After all, he's been doing this for a long time. The beauty is that when you're standing, you'll realize that you aren't sinking, but you're moving. Don't let your one thing trick you into believing that it has permanently paralyzed you. There is love for you. God even reminded you that nothing could come in between and separate you from that love. Not even your one thing.

Regardless of how many times our dog manages to jump back on the couch and how many times my wife and I walk over there to tell him to get off the couch, we still love life with our dog at the end of the day. There are consequences for some of the shenanigans he tries to pull, but never to the point where he is neglected and left out. He actually still runs to the door to greet me whenever I walk through the front door. Sometimes in the middle of another couch episode, I'm reminded of just how patient and loving God is with me. That patience and love are also waiting for you. All he wants is for you to come to him.

Recognize. Receive. Respond.

CHAPTER FIVE

FACING FAITH
WALKING IN THE WIND

The first few days of leading a mission trip to El Salvador were nothing short of terrifying. I had never been out of the country, let alone led a team of high school kids across the world with only a parent waiver saying I could. Amazing what a couple of signatures can do. I was responsible for making sure everyone was ready to go, financially and medically. The bank, airline, and doctors all signed off on us going, and after a long flight, we finally arrived.

I have to give a little backstory before I continue this story. When I was in sixth grade, I loved sports. I still do. Play sports. Watch sports. Any sports. Most of my days were spent in the driveway pretending I was Michael Jordan in game seven of the finals, trying to hit the game-winner. On this particular hot August day, I was playing football with some friends, and after playing for a while, I started to get really hot and dizzy. I had never experienced that before, and it didn't help that I had recently heard about a football player who died from heatstroke. Of course, that wasn't going to happen to me, but it was the first thing I thought of once the heat and dizziness hit. Ever since then, I've dealt with fear over my health. I think everyone has something they would consider their kryptonite, and that is mine. Everyone has that one thing that cripples and consumes them with anxiety and fear. Getting sick was one thing I was most concerned about on that trip. It was the one thing I knew for me might be the biggest walk of faith that I would take through the entire process.

The first official day in El Salvador was a training day. And by training, I mean dancing in preparation for elementary school assemblies. I can barely tap my foot and clap to the same beat, so you can imagine my choreography looked more like a comedy. At least the songs were in Spanish, so they didn't expect us to sing them too. About three hours into dance boot camp in a gym with fifty volunteers projecting body heat with only one oscillating fan to cool us all, my biggest fear wasn't dancing. As the leader of our team, I tried my best to power through until it got to the point that I knew I needed to sit down. The heat and dizziness were exactly like I remembered them when it happened the first time. I was starting to feel sick. With increasing chest pain, I took the walk of shame out of the gym and sat under the shade of a giant tree, like a big ball of fear and failure. Questions started spinning through my mind. Am I going to be able to live through this trip? Will I be able to recover? Will our team be disappointed? My body felt weak, but my fear felt strong.

Faith often feels easy when things are going well, but it's an entirely different ballgame when things don't seem to be going the way you thought they should. I'm sure you've felt that. It's hard to be certain when it isn't what you hoped for and to believe when it can't be seen. My plan for El Salvador at no point involved me being shook under the shade of a tree. Fear and anxiety have a way of leaving us shook. They are enemy number one to faith. They don't care about what you are doing; they only care about what they are doing to you. They work to make you weak and leave your mind to warp your reality by raising doubts. It's in those moments where we feel tested.

Faith is tested in the trenches. It is defined as it is tested. Taking the plane ride there wasn't a problem. I had done that plenty of times before. Walking the path of an unfamiliar country while being in pain was. Faith isn't some kind of wish that we have or make. Faith is the willingness to stand in, even when the strength of the challenges we face are staring us straight in our face. Those challenges often lead us to a decision—stay in your strength or become vulnerable about your weakness.

So where do we start when fear comes in and our faith gets shook?

We start by becoming vulnerable. We start by asking. We speak against the fear and doubts through faith. The disciples even asked Jesus to increase their faith when it came to challenge of consistently being willing to forgive someone who did them wrong. The best part for us is that when they did, Jesus didn't give them graphs or markers of what they needed to do in order to increase their faith. He told them what they could do if they had just even the simplest amount of faith.

Jesus isn't looking for us to add to faith as much as he is looking for us to activate our faith. We often substitute faith for the sake of our own strength. God already has strength, and he already knows what to do. All he's looking for is to show you what can be done when you simply lean in. He wants you to use what you have, even if it's a small amount. What is small can still go a long way.

POWER IN THE PRAYER TOWER

On the grounds of where we stayed in El Salvador, there was a large tower on a hill that overlooked the city. You couldn't miss it; this thing was enormous. The people from the area called it the prayer fortress. In this tower, teams of people would pray for the country and each other. There had been prayer consistently covered every hour for more than twenty years. Twenty-four hours a day. Three hundred and sixty-five days a year. My plan was to get to that prayer tower. Everyone who had been on this trip before told us this was a life-changing experience. I didn't know when they said that, just how much it would change mine. And that change would come through someone I least expected.

There's a verse that gives light to exactly what faith is. The rest of the chapter that includes this verse actually takes

you on a walk through the halls of faith. People who are recorded, went before us and are known for their faith. Heroes
like Noah, who by faith built a boat before any rain showed
up. Like Abraham, who, by faith, went to an unknown place
that God called him to that eventually was known as the
promised land. Like Moses, who by faith traded in his position and inheritance in Egypt to lead the Israelites to the
promised land. It's the same verse that I was ready to carry
with me to the prayer fortress that night. For some of us, we
manage to bring complexity to what is meant to have simplic-
ity. Faith is peeled back to just two things:

Confidence in what we hope for. Assurance about what we do
not see.

That we would be sure in the present of what we cannot see
and remain confident through that for the future. I came
ready to ask with the hope that I would have enough strength
to make it through the rest of the trip. I was still struggling
though with being sure of that because I couldn't see how the
whole picture would come together.

I think God gets excited even when we come with
what we have. We look at what we bring, and we say it doesn't
measure up. God looks at what we brought, and shows us
how much he can do with what we have. When we access
even the smallest amount of faith that we have in that moment, he gets ready to bring us the confidence and assurance
that we need. And he can do it in the most surprising ways.

I find that we often look for the plan and, instead, God brings us a person. For me it was a ten-year-old boy from El Salvador. I was about ten years removed from my last Spanish class that I took, so my understanding of the language beyond the basic questions you ask was pretty shaky. I couldn't understand much of what the Spanish-speaking people up in that prayer tower were praying for me, but as this little boy approached, and put his hand in the exact spot where my pain was and repeated the same two words over and over, I knew exactly what he was praying for. I can still hear his small but strong voice echoing the two Spanish words that I will remember for the rest of my life.

Tu Corazon.

Your heart.

God used a small kid that I would have never expected to bring about what it was that I most hoped for and anticipated. At that moment, every physical pain that was in my chest disappeared from my body. That wasn't all, though. Every single doubt and fear I was dealing with left with it, and I was filled with confidence and assurance. Chances are that whatever you are carrying, it's time to be vulnerable about its heaviness. There's a tremendous weight and pain in your heart about that decision or that experience. It maybe has left you with an elevation of your fears and a diminishing of your faith. It has crushed your confidence in the future and has attacked the assurance of the present. Sometimes we feel like the choice to deal with the pain will be less disappointing than putting that pain out there, believing in faith that something different will happen. I'm here to tell you that there is a rescue. Faith usually comes down to a matter of the heart. And if there's anything you've discovered by now, I hope it is that when you step out and walk your heart in God's direction, he doesn't disappoint.

As long as you didn't skip straight to this chapter, you've realized by this point that Peter was pretty well known for stepping out. Sometimes it was in faith. Other times it was skipped in stubbornness. Either way, God used it, and Peter learned from it. Faith is the decision to be courageous in the midst of challenges.

Often what we learn about God is found by being vulnerable and taking a step of faith even in the storm. Just before Peter took that big step, I want to take you one step back. There was a different storm that was stirring. It was a hunger storm. Five thousand of them, to be exact. The disciples tried to convince Jesus to send them away to a Chick-fil-A. The circumstances were great, and the supply was short. But Jesus had other plans. And that plan included building faith.

It's easy to retreat in a storm. Many times, we just want to step away or send our challenges away, and Jesus wants to show us how he comes through, even with the small portions of faith. He wants us to step in, even if it's small. The beauty and tragedy are that small things usually become big things. Sitting on what little you have will leave you with a big hole as you stare at exactly what you started with. Stepping in with what little you have will show you how much more is available. When it comes the time to decide what to do, Jesus will look at us and give us the choice about what we will decide to feed.

FAITH AND FURIOUS

Faith can be put in many places. It's just a matter of if it is the right place. We can put our faith in wrong places that are only feeding and growing our insecurities. Ever eat something that didn't agree with you? It's the worst. It may have tasted good at the time but leaves you crunched up in a ball with your knees up to your eyeballs in pain. We can put our faith in many places, believing it will be the feast that satisfies. Some of them we don't even think about. Some of them might even begin as good causes that become chaos later. We pour hours into our work because we want to be viewed as valuable. We get lost in a long unhealthy relationship because we live to want to be loved. We stress ourselves out tackling too much in the hopes of pleasing people. Feeding isn't hard to come by. It's just a matter of whether our faith is leading to what we are needing.

With five thousand witnesses sitting and waiting, Jesus took something small and illogical and held it up to heaven, in a way I imagine like Rafiki held Simba up on pride rock, gave thanks, and broke it. It's important who we are paying attention to and where we are putting our faith. If you want your faith to satisfy what you need, all you need to do is look to the one who does the providing. Faith is entrusting five loaves and two fish in the right hands and discovering a feast that satisfies more than could ever be known.

God is ready to give you the right stuff. God is always ready to bring you back a blessing bigger than what you even brought. All he asks is that you hand him what you have in faith. For the disciples, I'm sure feeding five thousand hungry people started off in fear, but when they brought what they had, it turned into full confidence, hope, and high-fives when they headed back to the boat.

We've all been through storms throughout our lives. Some storms have gone. Some have shown up more than once. Whatever your storm is right now, may not be the same storm that you were dealing with months, weeks, or even days ago. When a new storm comes, you're probably not even thinking about the last storm that you went through. The faith that helped you through the last storm is quickly forgotten in dealing with the new storm. It's easy for confidence to quickly become crushed, hope to feel hidden, and faith to fade. For the disciples, they forgot all in the matter of a few hours.

When you've just dealt with five thousand people, you need to get away for a while. That's exactly what Jesus did. I'm not much of a rock climber, and my first destination wouldn't be a mountain, but it was for Jesus. Jesus was so adamant about getting away that he made the disciples get in the boat.

No negotiations. It wasn't too much longer that those same disciples were getting beat up by a storm—waves, wind, the whole thing. I can barely handle a motion simulator ride, let alone getting tossed around with no seatbelt. Our circumstances have a way of making us feel the same way. That we are being thrown around like a chew toy for dogs with absolutely zero control. The more we get thrown around, the less we forget how far we've come.

We get focused on our fears and not our faith. On our present and not our future. On how this will make us break and not on how much we've already been brought through. We get so focused on what we are dealing with that it never dawned on us that Jesus is not that far away, waiting for us to be vulnerable and to come to our rescue. Some of the storms we have faced are drawn out because we don't reach out. Some of us stay in the storm simply because of the fear of what we might hear once we are rescued. No matter how long you've stayed in the storm, Jesus comes walking and not critiquing.

SIGHT YET SEEN

I don't have the best vision. When I was about ten years old, my parents took me for an eye test. I spent about forty-five minutes playing the one or two game. The one where the doctor gives you two options, and you can either lie, and everything can continue to look like a kaleidoscope, or be honest and shop for new glasses. My honesty walked out with a brand-new set of hardware on my face.

My fear, mixed with the fact that I could only see shapes once my glasses were off, led to more than my fair share of frightening moments. Many of them occurred at night when I had to take my glasses off. I was already terrified of being in the dark, so not being able to see just added to my fear factor. Every windy night outside my bedroom, a tree branch that looked like an oversized eagle's claw would tap on my window. It didn't matter how many days I looked out my window and saw tree branches, the minute it got dark, all I could see were claws that were slowly approaching me. It took everything in me not to run to my parents' bedroom. Pretty embarrassing.

I'm sure that same fear followed by the embarrassment that I felt was what the disciples felt once Jesus hit the water and walked towards them. I'm sure a couple of those disciples, out of fear, added to the volume of water once they saw what they thought was a ghost in the distance. In their defense, this "ghost" was walking on the lake. Fear will have you seeing and claiming crazy. Just a few short hours ago, Jesus was the guy they high-fived over a successful banquet. Now he's the ghost that is haunting them. Fear can blur faith. It will impair your vision and cause confusion to your confidence and hope. In our helplessness, the best option is to do what the disciples did and just vulnerably cry out, even if it is in absolute terror. And when we do, he doesn't call us cowards.

He tells us to take courage.

Jesus didn't even need to say his name after that. Once they heard courage, they knew they weren't dealing with a ghost.

In your greatest challenges, it is those same words that Jesus says to you. Courage, pointed in the right direction, clears the blur of fear. Fear will tell you to stay. Courage will tell you to come. To step out on the water when the boat is obviously more comfortable. To move from what is comfortable to the one who is known as the comforter. Living courageously requires vulnerability.

God is not concerned about our courage needing to look like us diving in head-first. Courage can look like us vulnerably putting out one foot at a time. He's more concerned that our step is focused in the direction of him. Ask Peter. He knows. He asked. He didn't want to just come toward anyone. He knew that the source of strength to step out was going to be because of who he was walking towards. It was only in the moment that he took his eyes off the one that brought him courage that he began to sink.

I've always wondered what it would be like to walk on water. I don't think it is what people say when asked what superhero ability they would want to have, but it would be great for a moment to feel what walking on water is like. They say that if you run at water fast enough for a split second, you feel like you are above water. I'm not sure if it's because I'm not fast enough or I don't have enough of a summer beach body, but I don't buy it. Unless you are superhuman, when we jump in water, we immediately begin to sink.

Most of us manage ourselves through our circumstances. We might sink but are able to stay tread and keep our head and breath above water. For a moment, Peter got the opportunity to know what it felt like to legitimately walk on water. To know what is was like to shuffle his feet above the waves. So what got Peter moving from a place of power and peace, to panic? You would think that when Peter started to sink that it was because he was afraid of the waves. But it wasn't.

It was the wind.

He saw the wind. I'm sure you just went back to read that to make sure you saw that right. You did. Of all the things that got Peter, it was the wind. We laugh, but what was true for Peter is often true for us. We get a little bit of momentum, having victoriously walked through something in our past that helps us recognize that God is faithful. You've walked through difficult seasons and are still standing. That the very same things that brought you fear are now the very same fears that you are walking above. Then the wind starts to speak.

You are dealing with a challenge in your life. Maybe it's an addiction, an answer that you were hoping would be different, a result that looked different than you planned. Chances are, when you face it for the first time, your fear is wrapped around the wind—what you can feel but cannot see. The end result that you have made up in your mind will no doubt happen. Sometimes it isn't the wave that crashes us but the wind that blows us over. It isn't the test that challenges us most, but the trick we believe that takes our faith. What we think we see can keep us from being vulnerable. It isn't the size of the wave but the sound of the wind that sometimes keeps us silent. You'll never get through this. The result will always be the same. You're going to sink to the point that you will never get out.

Faith is a matter of focus.

And just when you think all hope is lost.

The hand of rescue is readily reaching out to you at just the right moment.

WINNING DESPITE THE WIND

It's no surprise that in this life, we will fall short. For Peter, walking on water had to be one of the most glorious moments he ever experienced. I'm going to ask him what it was like when I get to Heaven someday. I wonder if the disciples were amazed that he walked on water or laughed at the fact that he fell in. Even though Peter fell short, at least he got out of the boat.

Sometimes you don't know what faith is like until you get out of the boat. Sometimes we'll walk, and other times we might sink a bit. We might fall short of the glory and security. The difference between having security is who you cry out to when you fall short. The difference between faith growing is who you focus on after you fall short. In order to be vulnerable, you need to know your struggle but see your savior. Remember, Jesus is ready to climb down mountains and walk through the same storm to catch you.

Some of us choose to not be vulnerable because we get caught up in what will happen once we get caught. Jesus wants to speak to your potential not your problem. Jesus says to Peter that he had little faith and doubted. Not to tell Peter what he is, but to remind him who he knows and what he really has. The only thing that Jesus will call you out on is why you didn't come to him. He knew Peter was a man of faith. He knew Peter was confident. He just stepped out of a boat.

You know someone is true to you when they will lovingly tell you the truth. You have far more in you than you know. You are probably doing better than you give yourself credit for. He wanted Peter to know, and he wants you to know. He would rather us use our faith and fall short, than to not use our faith and wonder what could have been. Faith pointed in the right direction always ends with him. The wind begins to die down. Faith begins to rise up. And that faith leads to celebration.

It always takes courage to step out and be vulnerable. But vulnerability grows your faith. It did for me in the prayer fortress on a mission trip in El Salvador. It did for the disciples feeding five thousand with five loaves and two fish. It did for Peter when he stepped out in faith in the middle of a storm and when he was sinking in a sea. Faith usually doesn't make sense. It feels illogical. It's supposed to because we typically are people who want to be in control. Faith feels like uncertainty, but it is actually security.

El Salvador was lifesaving and changing all in one. I'll never completely understand what I was dealing with while I was there, but since that moment in the tower, I never dealt with the pain I experienced again. I can't imagine what the rest of the week would have looked like if it wasn't for a small step of faith to a prayer fortress and the courageous and confident step by a small boy in El Salvador to pray for the pain of a man he had never met before. At that moment, what could have started in fear, ended in excitement and freedom to love and share life with the people in El Salvador. Sometimes we'll get hit by a storm. Sometimes we'll be sent into one. We can look at it as opposition or opportunity. You might be afraid. But courage is waiting for the taking in the middle of your fears.

Don't let the wind win. Take courage. Come out of the boat.

You might be surprised what you find when you do.

CHAPTER SIX

FRIEND WITH NO END
CRACKING OPEN THE ROOF

I have a friend named Nick. If we are talking movies, he is the Ferris Bueller of the friends that I have. We've been friends since high school, and through schools, states, jobs, and hairstyles have stayed connected. As time continues to fly by, one thing remains the same in my friendship with Nick. Every time Nick calls or texts me, I'm buckling in wondering what the next adventure is going to be. He always manages to find the most unique and out-of-the-box experiences. The last thing he sent me was an invitation to the annual raccoon feed. I didn't even know there was a raccoon feed and that it was annual. People are paying to eat something that I find feasting inside my garbage can. And Nick is one of the ones who is buying. I think everyone needs a friend who has a sense for the spontaneous. I can always count on Nick for an adventure. These adventures have usually led to some interesting and cool experiences. For one experience in particular, cool is an incredible understatement.

It was the first day of 2010. We had stayed up early

into the next morning after the celebration of an apple dropping to tell us it was a new year. My first day of the new year didn't have many plans to it. Sleep in until noon. Eat. Watch ESPN. The typical routine. Until Nick managed to get ahold of me, and before I knew it, I was out of a warm bed. Instead, we were standing on a beach in swimsuits, blowing hot air into our hands, contemplating if running into Lake Michigan was a good idea. After many running restarts, we finally took the plunge. We were like two ice cube trays that got put into a freezer. The only difference between us and ice cube trays is that ice cube trays don't have a choice about whether or not they end up in the freezer. We did. We ran out of the lake with two blocks of ice formed around our feet and a sense of fearlessness. Our bodies were freezing, but our hearts were full.

It was easily the shortest and most memorable swim of my life. I still get chills thinking about it. It doesn't take a climate expert to discover that water in January Wisconsin weather is going to make your teeth chatter until they want to fall out. I knew just from standing on the frozen sand just how cold that water might be. But it took a friend like Nick in my life taking me there to help me discover just how cold it was.

Spoiler alert. It was colder.

FRIENDSHIP FACTOR

Friends are great. They help you discover what you don't know. They even help you rediscover what you already knew but forgot along the way. They help you take courageous steps to sharpen you while still having concern for your safety. They point you in the right direction and run with you towards success and victory. You know who is for you when they take the plunge with you. We all need relationship. Ask Tom Hanks. Fighting for his future, he put his handprint on a volleyball and called it friend. The greatest discovery is knowing who is there for you when life gets difficult. It's often in the ability to be vulnerable that we discover the most. The greatest difficulty can be discovering who it is that you can be vulnerable with about what you are dealing with.

Friendship often feels like staring out from a distance and deciding whether you will run towards it or away from it. Friendship can feel risky. Often what makes that friendship risky is deciding when and whether or not you can be vulnerable. That you can share the parts of your life that most people may not know. Vulnerability is usually what determines the difference between a becoming a friend and remaining an acquaintance. Not everyone is worth telling everything that has ever happened to you.

Friendships have filters too. Those filters should be a factor because they can protect you from some of the messiness that can come with friendship. We all have questions when it comes to friendship. Will it have value, or will it leave me feeling cold? Will it be memorable or something I would rather forget? Will it leave me rejoicing or rejected? If you have lived beyond baby years, chances are you have experienced both sides of each of these questions.

Maybe at one point it's made you wonder if it would be easier to do life alone. Maybe you caught yourself at one point saying the popular social media baited phrase, "I'm doing me." The one that we really use to see who is for us based on how they do or don't respond. Andy Stanley has a phrase that I spend a lot of time saying. His phrase is, "If you live for yourself, you will have nothing to show for yourself but yourself. However, if you live for more than yourself, you will have more to show for yourself than just yourself." That speaks volumes when it comes to friendship.

Take it all the way back to the garden, and you'll realize there is beauty in friendship. God, the creator, created friendship. Unfortunately, we fell short with sin, and now our humanity can make friendships difficult. Thankfully for each of us, now is not the end. And God, who created friendship, sticks close and gives criteria that can provide us with vulnerable and fulfilling friendships.

One of the greatest analogies I have heard about friendships is that they are like elevators. They will either bring you up or take you down. Almost every person in any scenario would want friends that take you up and build you up. But for one immobile man in particular, he was thankful that two of his friends decided to lower him down.

FRIENDS THAT MOVE YOU

Many times, challenges can leave us feeling paralyzed. It did for the immobile man in a very literal way. He could not move his body. Many days he probably woke up with the little hope he had that this would be the day that he would be able to move. To stand up and walk. To run around. To do life outside of his bedside. To wake up and not have his challenges be the first thing he sees.

Your challenges may not be the first thing that you see. But they are felt. They aren't necessarily the ones that you notice physically, but you can feel mentally, emotionally, and spiritually. Not every vulnerability is visible. They weigh heavy on your life because they can easily go unnoticed to the eye, ears, and hearts of everyone else. It's easier to become content believing that this is just the way things are. It's harder to be vulnerable, believing and waiting to discover something better.

The immobile man probably woke up that morning just like he had every other day. With the routine and reality that this was the way his life would always be. Until a few men heard that Jesus was in town and decided to take their immobile friend and move him to experience and discover something different than anything he ever had before. The same can be true for you. You may have sat in the same place of pain. You may have stayed there long enough for it to numb you. But a new day and moving day happen to have come on the same day.

There is one life event that reminds me of who my friends are. It was the day that my wife and I moved. Long story short was that we were moving from an apartment to a house. We made our plans and went over them, again and again, to make sure it was in order. We showed up Thursday morning expecting to sign paperwork in order for us to move out that Saturday. Our landlord was expecting us to sign the paperwork because she thought we had already moved out. Not the kind of discovery you go looking for. She asked if the apartment was cleaned out. I don't know what hurt more, hearing those words or thinking about the hours of heavy lifting to get our lives packed up in one day.

Every U-Haul within a 25-mile radius knows who I am as I begged for a moving truck at any cost. I called every friend who I knew could stick with me through my worst. The harvest was plentiful, but the workers were few. We weren't mad. It was last minute. And with a few family and friends, we managed to get packed, moved out, and into a new place all in the same day. If any one of them called me up today in the same situation, I would be there in a minute. When you find a friend that is willing to do that, you, in turn, want to be a friend that is willing to do the same.

We can be moved to many things. Some of what we moved to in our past are the very same challenges that have paralyzed our present. Some may have a suitcase full of baggage, and others may have an apartment worth. That baggage we carry can often lead to the feeling of shame and responding with isolation. We've carried what is heavy and has no value for so long. Our fear is that if we ever shared it, it would cost us more than it would ever gain.

The first thing that you want in a friend that you know you can be vulnerable with is that they pay attention to what is close to you and listen to you without making a conclusion about you. They open you to the comfort and trust to speak under the surface. Often what sits on the surface isn't our struggle. It's what we use to mask our struggle. It's what we use to hide our weakness instead of choosing to admit it. A friend can pay attention. A friend worth being vulnerable with pays attention to you and cares for more than just what you project on the surface. They don't talk about the box that holds your baggage but lovingly ask you to show them what is inside. They are able to recognize you beyond the bed of baggage that you are lying in and see what you can become. At that point, you'll know that you found someone who doesn't only just see who you are becoming but also will believe in you enough to help you with the heavy lifting.

Letting people into our lives with more than just our limited details is difficult. As much as we feel paid attention to, we also need to be paying attention. Just as much as we may feel cared for, we also need to be careful. Paul summarized it in one of his letters to some people who were struggling.

"Do not be misled: bad company corrupts good character"
1 Corinthians 15:33

Your character is important to God because character is a key to victory. Your company will be important to you when your character is important to you. The difference between finding the friend who moves you and the one who may mislead you is found in how they serve. An acquaintance tells you what to do. A good friend goes with you. They will do what's difficult. Just ask the immobile man. His friends carried him onto a roof, ready to commit a breaking and entering for him.

A facial expression can say a lot of unsaid words. If you've ever gotten in trouble with your parent, teacher, or someone you love, it probably involved this to some degree. I can't imagine the facial expressions of those friends that just carried a man on a bed to a house full of religious leaders who wouldn't make room. Unfortunately, religious leaders were not exactly the friendliest people of their time. The law was more important than love. Being right was more important than being in relationships. Often deficiency was seen before destiny. It's the reason why they had to take it to the roof. They were driven to get this immobile man in the house and in front of Jesus.

Along the way, the weight and words of people will try and disappoint you into turning away from the house. The reminder that what you faced is what you will continue to face, leaving you with a fragmented future. To stop you on the outside of the house and deny you the healing happening on the inside. Don't stop and get defeated on the outside. A good friend will care about the inside. They will be someone who you can rely on when everyone else will deny; someone who will stick in the thin and thick. Find a friend who will help cut through the foundation of denial and defeat and lower you to Jesus. They help you discover and know a better future. And when you reach Jesus, he isn't giving you a facial expression that emphasizes your flaws. Instead, he's calling you a friend.

It was religious leaders that were always trying to trip up Jesus. But you can't trip up someone who is fully perfect. Jesus knew the thoughts of the men seated around him but paid attention to the vulnerable one in the room. And not only will Jesus pay attention to you, but he will also defend you. That's why the first thing he said was:

"Friend, your sins are forgiven."

I believe it's the same phrase he is still speaking to us today. It probably wasn't what the immobile man and his friends came for, but it was the start of the comeback. He won't just give you what you want but will give you what you need first. It can be easy for us to begin to believe that we know what is best for us. It may be good. It may be right. We come with a request. Jesus comes for the root. Jesus didn't want to just come and clear the visible pain but the invisible pain, too.

Ever pulled a weed out by the root? I'm not a professional gardener, but I've pulled some to the point of falling over. Taking something out at the root is tough and takes power. Jesus will show you on the outside but also wants to speak to you on the inside. He's a friend that chooses to do the tough work. He goes for the heart. He'll remind you that he has the power to be able to get both your shoulders and soul to stand. When we choose to believe, he will always do both. He's clearing your internal and external pain and making it permanent. Jesus will always give you more than what you bargained for; that's what good gift-givers do.

FRIENDS FOR YOUR FUTURE

Some of my greatest moments of celebration were centered around what was given to me. Most of them didn't occur at a birthday party or graduation where you sit and expect people to give you stuff. One of the greatest gifts I have been given wasn't something money could buy. Something that I didn't see coming but would change my perspective forever.

The final year of college turns into the time where you look at your future, and finding a job comes along with that. With student loans piling up, most people begin to stressfully look for something that they are both passionate about and will still pay the bills. A friend pursued me about a job he thought I should consider that was right in the place where I grew up. I made up plenty of excuses about why I wouldn't be a good fit for that position. I even threw out the excuse that I couldn't handle the cold weather. The same cold weather that I lived in my whole life. I'm sure you've done that at one point or another. My friend saw through all of my red tape and that my real struggle was that I didn't feel worthy of a job like that.

Little did I know that behind the scenes, my name was already brought up as a good candidate. All I needed to do was make the call. My friend stood at the front door of my apartment and wouldn't let me leave until I made the call. And it's the best call I ever made. A call that has gifted me more growth and guidance than I could have ever imagined possible. My destination could have looked much different if it had not been for the determination of a friend.

The greatest gift given to the immobile man was being carried to a conversation that turned into a celebration. Jesus tells the man to listen and gives him a three-step instruction to a new future.

Get up.

Take your bed.

Go home.

I'm sure the moment of strength coming back to that man's bones made all the effort that it took to get in front of Jesus completely worth it. He had spent many years sitting and waiting for a moment to walk again. Sometimes I can barely stand up after sitting through a long movie. And yet, he stood immediately. His moment to stand changed his entire journey and provided him the opportunity to show himself to his family as a new and free man. It took Jesus to heal him, but it took good friends to take him there. It took good friends who would cut a hole so a man's legs could function and his heart could be full. I'm sure the immobile man never looked at his bed or his friends the same way again. The bed was no longer a reminder of what is; it became a reminder of what was. It wasn't just a bed but a blessing. A symbol of celebration. It's probably why Jesus told him to take it in the first place.

I always wonder if they ever managed to repair the roof. I guess it's a question we will never know now, but can ask later. I do know that what was repaired in the room that day was worth far more than the cost of the repair outside of the room. Jesus is capable of anything, but yet he is inviting. He asks us to be a part of the journey that helps us see both ourselves and others come to a place of victory.

Jesus wants to partner with you. The enemy wants to isolate you. It's isolation that will ultimately keep someone from a destination. It's difficult to get to somewhere when you remain in the same place. Being vulnerable and asking for help just might be the first step to a different destination. Some of the greatest breakthrough of our brokenness will start by asking. Asking for help is healthy. It doesn't mean that you don't have anything to offer. The immobile man may not have had much to offer, but he offered something significant to the friends who were willing to carry him, cut a hole, and lower him through a roof. He figured out how to be a blessing even in his brokenness.

For most of my life, I have dealt with some seasons of social anxiety. I don't know if it's because I want to know what people are thinking, how they are thinking of me, or if

I'm a people pleaser. Truthfully, it might be a combination of all three. At points it has challenged me and chopped me at the knees. I'll talk with someone wondering the whole time if I am actually adding any value to the friendships or conversations that I have. I've spent weeks' worth of time listening and learning about the art of conversation. What I've discovered about friendship is the very same things Jesus did.

FRIENDSHIP IN PROGRESS

So how do I be a blessing even in my brokenness? The answer to this question is the beginning of this paragraph. If you want to be a blessing, you ask a question. Jesus was a conversational pro. He also asked a lot of questions. He asked 307 of them, and those are the ones that are recorded. He even answered questions with questions. Of all the questions he got asked, he only answered three.

Asking is how Jesus found his disciples. Asking demonstrates interest. Our brokenness can cause focus to be lost on others and only projected on the pain that we possess. Asking takes the focus off what I am dealing with and gives attention to others. Asking positions you to listen. And listening is one of the greatest blessings that we have to offer someone. It stops us from the speed of living and positions us to be still and learn.

The greatest love we have is to lay down our lives for our friends. To place and position our lives for our friends. The beauty in positioning ourselves is that it doesn't take skill but will. It doesn't take ability but availability. A blessing is being available, asking, and paying attention. You'll find that the friends you keep are the ones who do the same thing. That's vulnerability, and that's a reason to celebrate.

Friendship often is an ongoing and continuing work in progress. The ones who aren't willing to work are usually the ones we recognize over time as unreliable. Proverbs is pretty clear that unreliability leads to ruin. You may need to ask your friends if you have been reliable. You may need to reassess the ones who have been unreliable. But that isn't everyone.

There are friends that stick closer than brothers. Find those friends. Find friends who will go far with you and for you. Find friends that help you discover not just who you are but speak life into who you are becoming. That lovingly challenges you and helps you to stand up even when it doesn't seem possible. Ones who don't quit at the sight of a full house but climb the roof and cut it open. Find those that point you to Jesus and help you change for the better. And when Jesus tells you to get up and walk, don't choose to sit back down. Don't just find friends who take you to Jesus, but also be a friend that chooses to take people to Jesus. You don't need to break off the roof, but be willing to open the door. There will always be something great to discover.

I discovered something dangerously cold, jumping into nearly frozen water in January. I also discovered something new in my friendship with Nick. He didn't just tell me to jump in the lake; he went with me. We high-fived over our crazy and courageous test of strength, thanking God that we were still alive. A few years later, we went back again for a second jump. This time I discovered that onesies are warm but retain more water than I thought. You might call us crazy. We call us friends. The friends who cut a hole in the roof were probably considered crazy, too. But whatever you do, whether it is your friends for you or you for your friends, at the end of the day, let it be something that you and the people around you thank God for and let it be something that makes people like the ones who saw the immobile man stand up and say,

"We have seen very special things today."

CHAPTER SEVEN

GROWING FUTURE
MOVE THE MEASURE

Growing was important to me as a kid. So much that we had a designated chart in the house that would measure how much growth was happening. Maybe you had one of those. It was like a ruler, except it was giant and measured humans. I would run to this giant ruler frequently, with pen in hand, asking my mom to mark where I landed on the chart. Every time we consulted the chart, my mom had to remind me that standing on my toes was a direct violation of the rules of growth tracking. I wasn't trying to cheat, I was just committed to growth. Whenever that dashed line was above the one before, we celebrated. When it wasn't, there was a wave of disappointment and determination. Progress always made us feel bigger.

We all want to grow. Growing is an important part of living. As kids we looked to our parents to try and understand what growth looked like. Boys drew mustaches on their faces, had fake beard shaving sessions in the mirror, and wore ties over our cartoon t-shirts to make us feel like we were business class. Girls put on makeup, wore wedding dresses, and put themselves in their mom's shoes. We were having fun and also preparing and mirroring what we saw for our future in the present.

Growing is tied to our future more than we know. Whenever there is a season where we aren't thinking or focusing on our future, someone reminds us by asking the question, "When are you going to grow up?"

A mark above where we were shows we are growing and moving forward on the chart of life. And it isn't just for mustaches and makeup either. We want to see ourselves grow mentally, emotionally, and hopefully spiritually, which seems harder to notice.

Futures are God-given. He knows the plans he has. Jeremiah 29:11 reminds us that those plans aren't for harm but for hope. That's good news for us. Free will is also God-given. That isn't always good news for us. God gives us that free will out of the desire for authentic relationships. Our futures can be affected by our free will when it doesn't line up with God's will. Our human will can begin to hurt the hope we have for our future. It can put us in a place of panic over peace. Broken instead of bright. Our futures sometimes are affected by other's free will. Sin can set us back and make marking and seeing growth more difficult.

How do I mark my mind, emotions, and faith?
How do I know that I am growing?
How do I take steps that move me towards a bright future?

How do I have peace about my future?

What is the blueprint for a well-built future?

PROPERTY AND PRACTICE

Every strong house is built on a blueprint. And within that blueprint marks specific details about how that house is supposed to be built. The frame of a house shows its future. The foundation of a house keeps it secure. Every house has some particular sections that are specifically designed to support more of the heaviness of the house. Most houses have a lot of these. Our lives can have a lot of these. But when it comes to our future, I believe there are three support beams to a well-built future.

There are some charts that we love and others that we could do without. As a kid, that chart for me was the chore chart. This chart was made to show and help remind me of my responsibilities around the house each week. It was also used to give my parents a break. All I felt it was responsible for was reminding me that I didn't have as much time to do what I wanted and making me feel miserable. Sometimes I managed to do what was on the list and found the reward in the present.

There are many things we do not have an appreciation for in the moment. But seeing the growth makes it a different story now. I still find that reward today, just in a different way. I know how to do laundry, cut grass, and get to eat off clean plates without having to call my parents and ask for directions. It's cute when you're a kid and don't know. It's humbling as an adult.

We don't always get it right. It's true for us and true to what happened in the garden at the very beginning. What started as one command to not eat from the tree turned into 613 more commandments. Try building a future on that. Sometimes we have a hard enough time following ten. Thankfully, Jesus came and summed the law with two commands.

The chore chart wasn't always filled with stars. It had gaps. Those gaps showed what we decided not to be responsible for. Those gaps left us empty of rewards and full of consequences. The consequences reminded us of what could have been if we chose to be responsible. Taking responsibility changes results. You can change what you choose to take responsibility for. What happens now does not have to be the same result as the next time. It just takes a little practice.

Practice was the first word preached by Jesus about home owning to a crowd on a hillside. Homes were just the symbol. He was really talking about people. He doesn't start by telling them to break ground. He starts by telling them to listen. In order to know what to be responsible for, you have to know what to be listening for.

Practice usually isn't pretty. And it also isn't quick. Before you started reading this section, there were three other versions of this paragraph that got deleted. Practice can often be a long and ugly process. You'll also find that in my short-lived music career. And by short, I mean after three lessons with a guy who moved to Wyoming. How bad do you have to be for your teacher to move to Wyoming after three lessons? Every first practice session starts with the basics of what it is that you are trying to build. Before you can shred, you have to know how to tune. It's playing the same note every day for a week before you move on to the next note. Practice is focusing on where you can be. It's true for what you do. And it is also true for life. Futures that have foundations are centered around focusing on where God is taking you.

Nobody wakes up hoping for a ruined future. Our hearts plan for our version of happy, healthy, and wealthy. Futures can become blurry based on who we are listening to. Who and how we listen can leave us lost. Our lack of listening grabs shovels before we look at blueprints. We can take responsibility into our own hands, and the resources we are holding and building with can become beaten down and broken. Being vulnerable is being responsible. Vulnerability and responsibility are as much, if not more, about listening than talking. Listening will allow you to know who to put your hope into. Listening to God, who gives futures, will also give you steps to be responsible with your future. Jesus says to be willing to start up and step up to what he has set up. Responsibility is starting with knowing his words and putting his steps into practice. Responsibility is availability.

In any journey to better, there's a phrase that's been said to you. It usually comes along in your greatest moments of frustration.

Practice makes perfect.

Never has a sentence both frustrated and motivated us all at the same time. That statement reminds us of what it will take. Practice takes time and effort. We prefer quick. In a world where access is granted at the speed of a swipe, our frustration comes when we favor fast over foundation. Convenience has convinced us that time is something we are competing against. God doesn't want us competing against time but taking time.

Impatience, like a plan B, can get the best of us. Impatience to cut a corner for convenience becomes the evaluation and effort later when we see a crack in the foundation. Life can become overwhelming and filled with anxiety when all of our time is dedicated to moving at a pace that only produces pain. God created life for it to be enjoyed. Sometimes it will come with troubles. Sometimes they are self-inflicted. Being hard on ourselves often creates anxiety within ourselves. Our practice will never lead us to totally perfect, but it will lead us to patience.

Practice at points will sometimes be painful. Ever listen to someone who just picked up an instrument? Those first notes you hear make your ears want to run away. It will test your patience. But over time, as you spend time, the process produces something beautiful. Patience produces something beautiful in us. Patience doesn't pressure. Patience keeps your mind and emotions in check. Patience gives the ability to persevere. Patience activates faith. Patience helps keep the peace. And patience allows us to look back when we need to and realize how far we've really come.

Masterpieces take time. Vulnerability takes participation and requires patience. God knows we won't be perfect. You aren't expected to be Mozart when you start. God is simply looking for participation. God doesn't listen for failure. He hears the attempt. He doesn't want us to throw in the towel over our mistakes, but trust him, be patient in the middle, and triumph over them. Patience is often the difference between throwing in the towel in defeat or triumphing.

HANG ON TO THE TOWEL

It was around a kitchen table in 2008 that I almost followed through with a towel-throwing moment. It was the night before I was supposed to head up to college and start my journey toward the future I felt God had for me. I was in a single-parent home and headed for ministry, which isn't exactly where all the money is. So most of the year was spent hearing about finding scholarships and someone to help sign for loans in order to make that future possible. After working to make sure everything for the plan was in place, the signature fell out of place. I was sitting at the table, shrinking in my setback.

When our plan doesn't go as planned, often that's when the questions begin to flood in. Wondering if anyone believed in us because we see someone back out on us. The plan was laid out clearly and, all of a sudden, was blurry. All the work that was done felt like it meant nothing. The setbacks make us step back. Those setbacks seemed to make the towel seem bigger. And the setback sends us to plan B. As I sat at the table starting and already dreading my plan B, my aunt sat down and said something I will never forget.

"Sometimes you don't know if you'll walk on water until you decide to get out of the boat."

Wisdom came and reminded me not to give up on plan A. Wisdom tells us to have a loose grip on our plans and have a tight grip on God's plans. One phrase didn't change my whole situation. But it reminded me to remain open to what is possible. I dragged my feet a little bit. I could still see the towel. Before I knew it, I was standing in front of a college building with a little faith, no finances, and a future in sight. My first week was spent keeping everything in boxes just in case I was going to have to go back home. I don't know if I ever prayed so much in my entire life, but a signature came through, and I was able to stay.

Wisdom isn't always about having all the answers. Most of the time, it's understanding that God has all the wisdom and asking him for help. He actually says that is the beginning of wisdom. Our own understanding will leave us feeling like we are living below the bright future that is waiting for us. Our own understanding will also focus on us and try and tell us what we believe is best for us. Sometimes our own understanding wins out, but we play a game of odds every time our life leaves us with a decision. It's better to ask. In order to receive that wisdom, we must be humble enough to understand the limits of our own understanding and vulnerable enough to ask for wisdom.

When you choose wisdom, you take your own preferences and pull them out of the equation. You allow wisdom to tell you when and how to do what you need to do. Wisdom paves a straight path for you and points you right to where you should build. It's quicker to build on sand. It's better to build on rock. Ask Chevy. It's the reason they made their brand slogan "Like a Rock." They never made their slogan about sand. There's a reason for that. Nobody is looking to drive a truck or live in a house that is as solid as sand.

Sometimes it doesn't make sense. Sometimes it will require more work. But it will always be better. The wise thing and the right thing will always be the same thing.

CHARACTER MATTERS

If structure is the first thing in a strong foundation, character is the second. If the rock is the foundation, character is the present maintenance for the future. It's important to build. It's also important to keep and keep going. Building is just the beginning. Our futures often have a destination attached to them. We think of the places we want to go, the plans we want to achieve, and the people we want to take there with us. How we build can get us somewhere, but our character will keep it in place.

Some places in the house are harder to maintain. Just ask any parent. Some places in our lives are harder to maintain, the areas that tend to get messier faster. The places that turn into storage units for all the unwanted things we prefer not to see. What we choose to not maintain will turn into pain. Over time, they are the termites that come in to eat away at the foundation that is being built. Choose vulnerability and address the mess.

Everyone needs a few cleaning days. Not just for a house, but for the heart. It's the most important thing you have because the most important things come from it. You may be getting to where you are going, but guard your heart along the way. Home is where the heart is. Let people see your heart, but also be wise to guard it. Don't let what eats away, have a key to the front door. Find the people who won't walk inside only to make more of a mess, but the ones who will help you walk through the messes and keep the foundation strong. Find the people who ask instead of grab an axe and cut away.

Most of us are looking for peace and purpose when it comes to our future. We want a future that lives with peace on the inside and purpose on the outside. It's living a life knowing we are offering something that God has given us to be able to give to the world. The same world that comes with opportunities also can come with trouble. It's the very reason why Jesus recommended rock over sand.

How we respond to the trouble we face tells us where our foundation stands. The wind can tell us where we are, and the storm can show us if the foundation stands. There is pain when our peace and purpose are left in a pile. We feel overcome by the world. But that's when Jesus reminds us how He has already overcome. And if He's overcome the world, how easy is it for Him to open a door?

You don't need to see your storm as the end. Each storm is a chance to realize and reset. What we learn now can help us with what is next; that's growth. Your next victory can be seen in your present suffering. It can be scary to go back to God with what we have left, but when we choose vulnerability, we realize He isn't fixed on what is broken. He sees what is possible. Find the rock, pick up the strong pieces in the pile, and build again. Your peace and purpose will thank you.

Four years later, I walked across a college stage on graduation day with an uncomfortable cap on my head and a diploma in my hand. I felt like I won Survivor. I looked goofy but felt a sense of victory. The first week walking the halls of that college wasn't easy, but the future it brought was worth it. Futures take time. Building takes time. God knows the timeline for your future. Don't forake foundation and character in an attempt to fast-track your future. It will come.

In the meantime, take time and begin finding a solid foundation. Find out what it looks like to love God and love yourself. You and your neighbor will thank you for it. You don't need to keep setting up in the sand. Stop settling for sinking futures. Your future is worth more than sand. You may have built on it in the past, but your future doesn't need it. Be vulnerable to take what you know and move ahead. Look back, but choose to not live back. Reflect, but choose to not relive.

Don't settle on small pebbles. Build on big boulders. Solid foundations are found in those who choose vulnerability. By those who choose responsibility, built by those who are patient, and stays standing by those who exercise wisdom. And when you do, use the house to serve and not to show off. God is for your future. The creator of the universe went in and still is all in for you. You can't know the unknown, but you can see who you are becoming in it. Take the words that Jesus brought and build on them, and the result will always be stable. It takes vulnerability to step out when you aren't sure what you have. But wherever he leads, you will also come with enough resources for you. We might be building houses. God is building futures.

Sometimes in order to get to where you want, you need to recognize where you are. Building won't always be easy, but as you persevere, you will see the construction of character. And out of that character will come hope. Be vulnerable enough to say you've built on sand, but you're going to start to build on rock.

When you do, you'll be amazed at how much peace and purpose your future holds.

CHAPTER EIGHT

LOCKED IN FREEDOM
FEELING FRESH

My freshman year of high school, to date, was the most difficult year of my life. I'm sure there are plenty of people who could think of a million other moments they would rather relive than freshman year. Often we are able to deal with something that is happening. But it becomes difficult when something compounds into many things, and it becomes overwhelming; this was one of those seasons.

There's a reason why movies don't glorify someone's first day of high school. They go from one scene of being nervous but optimistic to the next scene, walking through the doors of possible war. Two college-looking seniors identify the helpless freshman trying to figure out his locker combination. Like animals, they wait for just the right moment to attack their prey. Just as the locker door opens, they pick him up like a human backpack and secure him inside his own locker.

I'm not just describing a movie. I'm describing the first day of my freshman year. I was coming from a small Christian school that was known for mid-week chapel services to a large public school that was known for its fight card. With no friends I knew and no backup, each waking day, I stepped with fear and wondered what could happen next.

While dealing with what was happening at school, I couldn't imagine there being another next. One thing was hard enough, but it was a string of things that amplified the hurting. The next thing didn't happen at a school. It hit closer to home. I owe a lot of who I am today to the time I spent with my grandma. She helped start a new chapter in the history of our family. Devastation hit when the words "stage four cancer" came out in a heavy and tear-filled conversation with her.

Life felt like it had plenty of lemons to squeeze enough lemonade for everyone we knew. But just when it felt like we were dealing with enough, there was another squeeze. The next one didn't hit close to home. It happened in the home.

Life that feels limited can make It difficult to know where to turn. Trying to be strong without speaking our need was leading to tension. Our family did the best job we could to try and walk through what was happening. But between these challenges and ones that existed long before, it led to separation.

The last page and a half may have been a lot to take in. It wasn't just a lot for me to take as I was living it, but as I was writing it too. Some of you may have picked up this book because of the title. Maybe you're like me, and you pick up books because a cool cover catches your eye. Regardless of the

reason, there's a chance that you have walked through challenges. Maybe they are like the ones I just mentioned. Maybe
your story has different situations from mine buried in the
lines of the pages. Some of the situations passed by. Some of
the situations are still there.

You felt stuck trying to understand what hope was
leftover when all seemed lost. The questions of where to turn,
who to turn to, and why it was even worth trying came to
mind. Despite every best effort, it felt like life kept dealing
losses to the point where it wasn't surprising anymore. Whatever it looks like, chances are you were or are looking for the
same thing I was.

A WAY OUT

When we're looking for a way out, what we're really looking
for is freedom. Something that doesn't make us feel like we are
living hunched over but lets us live with our head up. A life
that is filled with joy instead of being jaded. Living hunched
over limits what you can see. Living exhausted limits what's
possible. What's failing feels limiting. And what's limiting
makes freedom feel harder to find.

So how do we experience freedom when life seems to be failing and limiting?

It was a bunch of disciples who got hit with hard
news that tried to figure out freedom. The news we don't

understand usually is the most shocking. I think there's more than one reason why it can be called breaking news. The hard things that we never believe could happen move through our ears and into our hearts, leaving us broken. For the disciples, it was what they heard from Jesus. That the man who told them to follow Him, whom they grew close with, wasn't going to be around on earth forever. He was headed back to be with His Father.

It's easy to try and take control. The disciples did the same thing. They didn't understand why, so they tried to take control. They didn't even ask Jesus for the reason why he needed to be with his father. They skipped asking Jesus why and looked to each other to figure out what to do. All they really had to do was ask.

We like to be in control of life. We don't like when life feels out of the grasp of our control. We like to be in control of the plan. When the plan becomes hard to understand, control is often the reaction. We try and handle all the smaller pieces because we can't see a bigger plan. Feeling like the plan is slipping has a way of getting us to react through doing instead of responding by asking.

We do something because fear has left us looking over our shoulders, wondering what could be coming next. Worry makes us believe there isn't a way out. Anxiety convinces us that what we think is what will actually happen. Our hurt tells us to take situations into our own hands. Those feelings are often what are working against us to limit us. To make us believe that there isn't a plan for us. Being convinced and consumed by those feelings is what robs freedom.

GROUND CONTROL

What we carry and how we try to control what we have can leave us feeling captive. Being in control can eventually show us what we are controlled by. Being in control locks us into the box of our own limitations. Limitations can leave you feeling captive. Captivity can leave you numb.

Jesus talked about troubles. He said we would have them and told the disciples as he was about to head out.

"In this world you will have troubles" John 16:33

It doesn't get me excited. I appreciate the honesty, though. Life comes with challenges we can't control. Ask the guy that gets stuck in traffic. He would pick a clear freeway if he could.

Life brings circumstances that are beyond our control. But how we respond is within our control. Taking control of what you can't often ends in losing control of what you can. Control what you can and give the rest. The best part is what comes after that. While there are things that are overwhelming, Jesus has promised us he has overcome them.

The hurt may be what is happening right now. But it does not have to be the end. Where we take our heart is how the hurt gets handled. Where to turn, who to turn to, and wondering if it's even worth trying no longer need to be the questions. The invitation is being given to you for something different, and Jesus is waiting for the call.

When we give control instead of taking control, we gain control. Not always to the outcome but to the inside. Giving control gives the space to grieve. Comfort comes when you give your grief.

Everyone at some point in their life has experienced grief. If you can't raise your hand to having dealt with some type of suffering in your life, then, chances are, you might be a robot.

Grief and suffering are not high on the list of what anybody chooses to walk through in life. We all like to picture ourselves more as the Rocky Balboa that has his arms raised at the top of the stairs than the one that is trying to pick himself up off the mat. The mat can be where we are at. We all will experience grief in our lives. Acting like grief was never there leaves us, over time, with more pain that we can bear. Instead of letting pain pile up, it's important to get up and go somewhere with our grief. Where we go with that grief can determine where we are headed. And where we take that grief often shows us if there will be freedom or further limitations.

It can be easy for us to start to bring our grief to whoever and whatever we think will take it. We bring our pain to people who don't know how to handle it. We grab the substance that doesn't provide a solution. We post on social media, waiting to see who or if anyone will react to it. It's easy to just cry out for help when we are grieving. It's important to not only cry out for help, but for health. Help from the wrong places can create more harm. Help in the right places leads to health. When you are healthy, you are able to live freely.

TRUTH UNLIMITED

It was my limitations that led to a moment with Jesus. A climactic moment of everything I was facing gave me an invitation to freedom. Life had become so heavy that all the limitations that felt like they were hovering over me convinced me there was nothing more to live for. Limitations will tell you that what you have is all that you can hope for. In my hopelessness and helplessness, I was prepared to take my life in my own hands.

Just before I was ready to follow through, I was invited to a youth group that was having service that night. I had been a church kid growing up, but difficult times had pulled me away from what I once confident knowing. I was skeptical that it could do anything for me, but decided to go as a last chance for something different.

That night I headed into service with plans for the next day already in my mind. The minute service started, though, something was different. Even though I had been suffering, I was experiencing something different than what I had been used to feeling. Jesus said there was one thing that would set someone free.

The truth.

That night the truth managed to melt what was numb, and I began to walk through grief. We can get caught up in the lies that our situations tell us. But the truth will cut through, if you let it. Moving toward truth with your grief is the first step. You'll know when it's truth because it doesn't just lovingly tell you who you are but shares with you the beauty of who you can become.

Sharing truth is next. Find the person that will help you to health. For the disciples, it was Jesus. He was standing right in front of them. For me, it was someone who was in charge of leading that youth group who found me in the back row and allowed me to share with him what was hurting. It was someone who was being like Jesus. When circumstances are grieving you, look for someone who will listen to you and then join you. As you take the time to talk, you'll find that your grief begins to cut in half. Talking and sharing honestly, begins to make room for freedom.

Truth didn't change all my circumstances overnight. Circumstances don't provide shortcuts. The way through is usually the way out to freedom. Freedom is a choice. It'll require you to stand firm in it. It didn't change having to walk into school on Thursday. It didn't change the hearts of those who were there that had hurt me. It didn't change a cancer diagnosis. It didn't change divorce. But it changed my heart. It changed the way I woke up. It changed the way I walked.

My grief turned into belief.

Limitations will tell you that all you see is all that you have. Belief tells you that there is more to be found than what you see. When life happens, trying becomes easier than trusting. But it's trust that allows you to do what you are able to do and let go of the rest. It's telling God that He gets it and that you're giving it. It's giving God control, knowing He knows best. When you put your trust in the one who sets free, you'll find yourself free. No gimmick. No game. Just gain.

By the end of my freshman year, I found more freedom than I ever thought was possible. The first was a shadow of where cancer used to be. My grandma overcame the odds, and we got many more years with her than we thought we might get. Not knowing how it could ever be afforded, I received a huge financial break and was able to attend a safe private school. The youth service that I was skeptical about became a second home for me. I was surrounded by a community that helped to keep me healthy.

Nothing better can begin when we only cling to the past. Health is possible when you choose to become vulnerable. You might have a tight grip on the past, but you can let it go because what is promised to you is new. Challenges can be a chance to see how God shows up and shows off. The disciples found that out. They walked through their season of grief, and eventually, it became their joy. Trying to keep Jesus around would have meant missing out on a greater plan. Letting go actually gave life. And that plan is still paying out. The son can be set free because freedom was paid in full. He's paving roads where it is wild and bringing life from waste. I never thought my challenges could benefit me until I walked across a graduation stage with a degree and the opportunity to speak to those same students who sat in the back row just like I did.

If you still find yourself in the valley, walk through it. And while you are, there is no need to fear. You may feel like you are suffering as you are walking. Remember, those same challenges that you are walking through are growing you. Challenges can grow you if you let them. It feels sacrificial now, but it's gaining interest for later. Take the invitation. Find the places that bring truth. Find the people who listen and love you to health. Be honest about where you are. What you face doesn't have to last forever. Don't let it convince you that it limits you. Freedom is coming. And it's not as far as it seems.

CHAPTER NINE

LICENSED AND DETERMINED
PURSUING PURPOSE

For some, it's the one they will always remember. For others, it has moments that they wish they could forget. Although, those problems they had at the time might have made for some good memories to remember today. Some people had so much love for the first one of these that they owned that they went on the hunt to uncover another one just like it so they could reminisce on the good ole days.

Still haven't figured out what I'm talking about?

I'm talking about someone's first car.

Mine happened to be a 1994 baby blue Toyota Corolla. Now, this car was probably prime and sublime when it was first released in all of its four-cylinder glory, but when I received this baby blue road machine in 2007, it already had some stories to tell; 268,000 to be exact. And that was just the start. Some of those stories so far had led to a missing passenger side-view mirror, likely from a war with the edge of a garage. A missing hubcap that probably was sitting in a landfill somewhere. And a huge crack across the entire windshield so big that it looked like it was tail whipped by a T-rex. Every time I would get on the freeway, I could expect that once I started driving over fifty miles an hour, I would be greeted with a violently rattling steering wheel that made me feel like I was off-roading. Despite all of this (and this was just the start), the engine was strong, and this car had no quit in it. Up until its last exhausted breath in 2009, this car each day served the purpose of getting me to where I needed to be.

We all have a certain amount of mileage that we've lived out. For some, it is more than others, but regardless of how many years we have lived, we all have lived out a journey up until this very moment. Maybe some of our lives feel a little bit like my baby blue Toyota Corolla. Situations in life have felt like they've beat up our structure. Disappointments have left us feeling a little dinged and dented up. The mileage that we've racked up lately has left us tired. When all of those start to show, it's easy for our purpose (or gas if we are still talking in car terms) to go empty and decide to park it somewhere with little to no use. To look at everything that exists on the outside and determine that there is no purpose or value on the inside.

So how do we not let the accidents we've experienced in life completely crash our purpose? How do we fire up our internal engine again, take our lives out of park, and realize that we have a purpose? How do we not let what is on the outside distract us from the beauty and purpose that exists on the inside? As incomplete or lacking as it may look right now, the beauty is that God, who we often regard as the creator, is also a great mechanic. If you let God tune-up your sense of purpose, I believe it'll tune-up your life. Are you ready for a tune up?

PARDON MY PRESENCE

If there were cars back in Biblical days, I imagine that Gideon would be rolling in my Corolla. Gideon's felt his purpose was in the poverty category. When an angel of the Lord appears to Gideon, he's threshing wheat, which is probably the equivalent of a minimum wage job back in Biblical days. But this angel was about to put Gideon's limitations on the threshing floor and bring him revelation.

The first thing to reclaiming our purpose again is to separate our limitations from the revelations. It's easy to look at the exterior of our lives and determine that it must match what exists on the inside. The beauty is that God sees what is on the inside and calls you by the purpose He sees in you that you haven't seen yet in yourself. You see worry and weakness, and God sees a mighty warrior.

Ever give your car a nickname? Maybe you call your car "Hank" or "Lucy" (sorry to anybody with those names reading this book and for determining that your name could also be the nickname of a car) because it seems to give your car a human-like personality. The car I currently have I've nicknamed "The White Tiger" because, you guessed it, it's a white car with two little black stripes on the side. It's a common everyday six-cylinder car. But with that nickname it has led me to believe in a potential unlike any other six-cylinder car I've had before. Just ask my wife. She sits in the passenger seat when I drive. God has nicknames for us too. This angelic encounter leaves Gideon with a new nickname.

Mighty warrior.
Yes, the poverty-stricken wheat thresher.

I have to imagine that Gideon thinks they have the wrong guy. I know I would. That just feels like a ton of responsibility. It's hard to feel like a mighty warrior on your own, especially when you are now just realizing that there might be more purpose in you than you first saw. Where God gives purpose, He always involves a promise. And that promise is Himself. That in your journey of purpose, God's presence is sitting there, showing you how to get there. Gideon doesn't just get purpose; he gets presence.

I'll be the first to admit that as I look for purpose in my own life, I have felt the pain and silence of what feels like an absence of presence. It's the reason why this book, which I have felt led to write to help give people hope and purpose, has been parked and restarted so many times due to feeling a lack of presence and questioning the promise. Much like us, Gideon doesn't just immediately receive this promise and purpose. He calls it into question. Or questions. Check out this list.

"Pardon me, my Lord," Gideon replied, "but if the LORD is with us, why has all this happened to us? Where are all His wonders that our ancestors told us about when they said, 'Did not the LORD bring us up out of Egypt?' But now the LORD has abandoned us and given us into the hand of Midian."
Judges 6:13

Don't let the two question marks fool you because there are many more questions buried in this response.

These questions are some of the same ones we ask ourselves. Our enemy can come in the form of believing the lie that God has been inactive. To believe that God has abandoned us. Gideon is speaking of Midian, but I think, for us, we are speaking of median. You probably remember this word best as a middle school math term for finding the middle point. Not exactly the word anyone wants to attribute to their purpose. Nobody wakes up each morning hoping that they live each day in a middle-of-the-pack kind of way. But for some of us, while it's not what we want, that statement feels more real than we would like to admit.

We wonder if we have the strength to do the next purposeful thing in our present because the wonders of the past seem like a distant memory. The fact is that while I could use the past to complain and be frustrated about the purpose

I feel I don't have in the present, I would much rather look back on God's faithfulness in the past and realize what is possible by living with purpose in the present. Instead of getting frustrated, get focused. Don't let the season of your own inactivity or feelings of inadequacy keep you from the great things that are waiting for you.

GAS TO KEEP GOING

Remember when you got behind the wheel at driver's ed? Maybe some of you would rather not based on who you had to drive with. I feel you on that one. Every lesson at my driver's ed class required one hour of hands-on driving followed by one hour of watching other driver's ed students, who you didn't get to choose, drive you and the instructor around. There was something that just didn't feel right about putting your life in the hands of someone random who only had a learner's permit like you. Thank God for the gas and brake pedal in the passenger seat where the head instructor sat.

My first behind-the-wheel observation lesson featured a student who sat in the driver's seat and couldn't identify which pedal was the gas and which one was the brake. Needless to say, we spent the rest of the lesson in the driver's ed parking lot, and my afternoon was spent at the chiropractor's office getting adjusted. We didn't go anywhere, but at least we started. One of my favorite quotes that has stuck with me and has been a verbal lightbulb of illumination and motivation for my life has been.

"You don't need to be great to start. You just need to start and God will do something great."

Now that I think about it, it is definitely scarier when you apply it to situations like learning how to drive or juggling fire. But that quote still manages to ring true no matter what you do. Most of what we see people do that is great would never have become great unless they had started.

When it comes to living with purpose, I think many of us would admit that we would love to be strong and make a meaningful impact right away. Some of the hardest parts of moving toward living with purpose is that we want to be stronger and have more than what we presently possess. It can be a great motivator to step on the gas towards growth, but it can also be demoralizing and cause us to put on the brakes and stay right where we are. The beauty about God and the blessing for Gideon in him walking toward the purposes that were prepared for him is that God can make much out of what to us seems minimal. Like the quote I shared with you earlier, God says something to Gideon that I think stuck with Gideon as motivation to keep going.

"The LORD turned to him and said, "Go in the strength you have and save Israel out of Midian's hand. Am I not sending you?"
Judges 6:14

Go in the strength you have. Based on Gideon's previous questions, work history, and position in the family, he doesn't see a whole lot of strength in himself. But God does. He is great at seeing the greatness in us that comes long before we've even started. And the strength it will take that goes beyond the strength we currently possess is what God already possesses. God tells you to go in the strength you have because you can be confident that when He has spoken to you about a purpose to step into, He will be behind you with all the strength you could ever need at your disposal as He is sending you.

We've sat out on some of the purposes that we are meant to step into simply because we've bought into the belief that we need to have a certain amount of strength in us before we can take the next step. Don't let what you think will never be enough keep you from taking the step with purpose because on the other side of your step, you may find out there was enough. It will take vulnerability to go in the strength you have, but remember that God can use what is currently in your possession. It may not be Israel, but the world is waiting for you to step into your God-given purpose. And when you still aren't sure about if that purpose is possible, God will remind you all over again that He is with you.

PURPOSE WITH TRACTION

There was one thing that made my Toyota Corolla more dangerous than it needed to be: the tires. I look back, and wonder how I managed to stay alive through multiple Wisconsin winters with that much lack of traction. These tires were so bald I could have started applying Rogaine on them. One winter day on my way home from school, I lost traction and slid through an intersection. Backward. I managed to channel some stunt driver instincts and not hit anyone around me, but I managed to lock eyes with the person driving behind me as our cars ended up facing each other. I found out quickly how important traction is, and the difference between Vin Diesel and me is that I had to change clothes after my stunt.

Maybe some of you have read this chapter up until this point, and you're thinking, "Yeah, the purpose thing is good and all . . . but I'm wondering if what I'm doing right now is really my purpose."

For you, maybe it feels like the specifics of the process surrounding your purpose are still in question. Two things.

1. I'm glad you thought that because it means you want to live with purpose.

2. If you have thought that, it means you are alive. And if you are alive, it means that God has a plan and purpose for you.

You probably have realized by now that purpose doesn't all happen overnight. It would actually make the rest of our lives boring if it did because we wouldn't have much more to feel like we could live for. Finding purpose is a journey for a reason, so let's not get lazy, but let's also not rush into it. Rushing into something that ends up not being our purpose can actually feel worse because it's like hearing the GPS remind us that we have to reroute and go back to where we originally were meant to be. The uncertainty we have about our purpose is the same thing I felt about my tires. Does it have traction?

Usually, the best way to figure out if your purpose has traction is to run your fingers through the tread. That's easier said than done when what we are dealing with is more imaginative and figurative than it is physical. To know if the purpose has tread is to put it to the test. It's exactly what Gideon did. It is what many people now know as his fleece. As Gideon asked God for a sign, he was prepared to bring him an offering. And the best part is while Gideon was committed to bringing the offering, God was committed to waiting.

Every future purpose has a present process. Take a look at what is around you that you are gathering and offering. Gideon grabbed a goat and some bread to see if the purpose and plan had tread. For us, it will probably be our time, our efforts, our skills, our resources, and ultimately, ourselves. It's the things that are currently in our possession. Part of the process will likely involve us pausing for moments on what we are currently doing so that we can determine what we are purposed to be doing. Gideon was a wheat thresher, but, at some point, he had to leave the threshing, so he could take the flour to start baking the bread. Each process of purpose can look different. Pay attention to the instructions and walk them out in order.

FIRED UP AND POURED OUT

At some point along the preparation process comes a time to put what's being offered on the altar. It takes vulnerability to put what you have to offer on the table. To put it before God and find out if it is the purpose that is meant to be pursued. To see if what is placed before God has the traction to be driven on. Gideon was told to pour out the broth, put the meat and bread he prepared on the rock, and wait for confirmation.

Let's talk about the broth. I'll be honest, I'm not a huge fan of broth, so pouring it out isn't much of a problem for me. But if we are talking about moving towards recognizing our purpose, there are many things that act as broth in our life. The literal broth would be easy for me to pour out, but I have a harder time pouring out some of the figurative broth that exists in my life. It's the things that really don't push us towards purpose. It's what is liquid in our life. And it might be time for us to pour out the broth. To let go of the things that are unnecessary so that we can further focus on what is.

Every purpose in life should have two focuses: fire and honor. You could also call it passion and position. It's the two things that Gideon found that day that would set him on a traction-gripping, purpose-filling trajectory. As he placed what he prepared on top of the rock, it was consumed by fire.

With what you can offer, position yourself in God, and see God ignite and consume you with passion. Let the fire that comes from God be the honor that is lived out for God. Let the destination God has pointed out to you become the drive that begins within you.

My baby blue Toyota Corolla taught me a lot of lessons over the years. Some were dangerous and difficult, but all were valuable. To the world that shared the road with me and to the many people that passed me on the freeway, they probably looked at what I drove and kept their distance because my car seemed to be only one more mile away from collapse. I don't blame them. I sometimes thought the same thing. That baby blue Corolla probably wasn't at the top of anyone's dream car list. Most of the cars that were out there probably cost more and held a higher value. I know that for a fact because I paid one dollar to purchase that car. (Thanks to my aunt and uncle for the deal!)

Regardless of how anyone else might have felt, I was excited because I knew that car gave me a new sense of purpose and opportunity. At the end of the day, if I was going to the same place as someone else at the exact same time, they possibly could have gotten to the destination faster, but ultimately that car would get me to where I was going. It got me to school to learn, to work to earn, to hang out with friends, and at some point, back home.

You might feel like your purpose right now looks a little like my one-dollar Toyota Corolla, but just because on the outside, it doesn't feel as able or valuable, on the inside, there is a useful and purposeful engine that is waiting to roar. That engine is worth starting up because while you may not feel like you're getting where you want to go as fast as you would like, when you go in the strength you have, God is guiding you, and you will eventually arrive at your destination.

Gideon saw God fire up (literally) the engine of purpose in his life. It's difficult sometimes to know that you are about to enter into a journey that seems longer than the vehicle can take you, that the purpose seems too big for the person. When you start to worry and wonder if this purpose is truly meant for you, God says the same thing to you that He said to Gideon.

"Peace! Do not be afraid. You are not going to die."

The journey in purpose may not always be easy and can get a little discouraging. At times, you might catch a flat tire. God has plenty of tires to spare. Throw one on and keep going. You might slide through an intersection. Thank God that He kept you safe, do a three-point turn and keep moving forward. Whatever you do, make sure that you wave the starting flag instead of the white flag. And let these words carry with you as you put the key in and ignite your purpose. God is bringing you peace, purpose, and power.

It's time to start your engines.

CHAPTER TEN

CROSSING THE STREET
LIVING VULNERABLE LEADERSHIP

I remember the day I was offered the position. It was highly coveted by many and was presented with a seriousness of life or death that I had never experienced in my life. I accepted the power of this position with great responsibility and an intensity to live above and beyond the call of duty.

I started the year serving as the eighth-grade crossing guard.

Sorry if this lead up felt a bit anticlimactic. But let me tell you this job had its perks. Each day as the final school bell was about to ring, I would get out of class a little bit early to go to the storage closet and grab the official crossing guard outfit, which consisted of an orange neon vest and a large stop sign. I would make my walk down to the early elementary building and face the danger of walking into the middle of the road with nothing more than a red sign facing the approaching cars and leading small children with their parents on the passage of safety on the other side. Parents thanked me. Teachers appreciated me. I was unstoppable with a stop sign in my hand.

This chapter and the previous chapter (Which hopefully you have read. If not, bounce back a few pages and check it out.) go hand in hand. We spent much of our time in the last chapter talking about the vulnerability it takes to recognize and walk in our God-given purpose, which leads us into this next chapter. Leadership.

While it might not look like standing in the middle of a street holding up a stop sign, I think many have a desire to be a leader. We want to be able to positively and spiritually impact and influence the lives of those around us. We hope that as we step into the middle of the purposes that God has given us, we can look back and see that there are people who are willing to follow us.

Leadership usually comes when you consistently live in specific purpose. The more time you spend in the purposes that God has given and called you to, the more you may find people taking notice and beginning to follow behind you. How you walk in purpose usually becomes where you go in leadership. So how do I know I'm walking this purpose in the right direction? What does it look like when purpose and leadership begin to intersect? Questions have a great way of putting our focus in place. Speaking of focus, let's zoom in on that for a second.

SHIFT AND SIFT

My wife came to me recently with a kind, yet honest, and not so startling conclusion: I have too many pairs of shoes. As much as it hurts to type what I am about to share with you . . . she's right. I enjoy shoes, and even though I don't keep my shoes immaculately clean and kept in the box, at this point, I'm probably a shoe collector. In my defense, I haven't paid full price for a single pair of shoes that I own. I currently have shoes in a handful of places in our house, and if I were to put them all together, I could probably make a small Foot Locker. It's become clutter.

Clutter has a way of keeping us from clarity. It's true of my closet, where most of my shoes are, and it's also true of leadership. Clutter can keep you from focusing on what is in front of you and functioning at your best. The clutter can come in a variety of ways. Your schedule. Your thoughts. Your emotions. Your Netflix watch list. Now, that's not to say any one of these things is bad, but it becomes unhealthy when it starts to clutter the leadership that rests within you. Stepping into leading sometimes requires shifting and sifting.

If we go back to our guy Gideon, who is just starting on this journey of moving out from his wheat threshing shoes into leading an army of Israelites shoes, his leadership journey starts unlike most leaders of an army. I don't know much about armies, but with the little I do know, I can tell you this—you want to have as many in your army as you can, and you do not want to be outnumbered by your opponent. Gideon's army started at 32,000 people. That seems like a lot until you realize the army across from you outnumbers you four to one (the other side had 128,000 people just to save you the math problem). So, you can imagine Gideon's surprise when God tells him that he has too many men. The first round of sifting cost Gideon 22,000 people and the second round of sifting cost him another 7,700 people, leaving Gideon with only 300 people. Yikes. I can't imagine how Gideon or those 300 people felt knowing they went from being outnumbered 4:1 to almost 427:1. It may look like Gideon's leadership is getting off to a grave start, but God knows exactly what He is doing.

I mentioned before the things that can clutter and get in the way of leadership within you, and I left one out that is all too common. For Gideon and his army, it was the pride of believing they would win this battle all on their own. The bigger we get doesn't always mean the better off we are. The more we squeeze into our life does not always mean that we are making the most of our life.

Your first step in leadership may require putting the lens back in focus and allowing God to adjust and sift through what is keeping you from operating in the leadership that is within you. Those adjustments can be difficult. And some of the decisions we may need to make at the moment will make us waver and wonder if we are truly equipped as a leader. The beauty is that God can do so much with our focused few than with our unfocused much. And when you get focused on the few, you'll begin to better see what God is doing in you.

WAKE UP CALL

I will be the first to say that I am not a morning person. I'm trying to get better at waking up early, but I enjoy staying up late, and I like my sleep, which makes for a pretty bad combination. The day can be pretty loud, but when it gets to that point in the night, I like to have it quiet. I enjoy putting my head on the pillow after a long day, closing my eyes, and drifting off into a deep sleep. If God gives me a wake-up call in the middle of the night, it must be pretty important. You also know you're an important person if I am willing to step out of the slumber of my sleep for you. I don't know if Gideon was a morning person or not, but God gave him a wake-up call to get up and go down into the camp of Midian. It's easy in leadership to start drifting into sleep when it gets quiet. To close our eyes and relax on the purposes and plans that God has put in front of us. It may not be a wake-up call in the middle of the night, but it is important that in the moments when it feels quiet, we remain with our eyes open and paying attention. Rest is important in real life and also important in leadership life, but don't get caught putting on the sleep mask and the noise-canceling headphones. Be ready at a moment's notice to move. We know from Gideon's wake-up call that God could have us move at any moment. Some of the most important calls happen in the quietest of moments.

In leadership, paying attention when it's silent often allows you to hear what is being spoken to you the most clearly. You hear best when there's the least amount of noise. Ever been outside in the middle of the night? Most of the time, all you get is the crickets doing their late-night concert. It's the reason why some of my best dreams have happened in the middle of the night. And I'm not just talking about the ones that happen with my eyes closed in that deep sleep I told you about.

I enjoy having conversations about dreams. Not just about my own that I've had while I was either asleep or awake, but also hearing about the dreams other people have. You can get a really good conversation out of talking about dreams. Leadership is more than just having dreams. A big part of leadership is also listening to others. It's the reason why there's scripture about being slow to speak and quick to listen. You never know the great things you find when you take the time to listen.

For Gideon, He got in on one of those dream conversations, and that conversation became Gideon's confirmation for the rest of the army he was leading. Listening can become the difference between starving and eating, staying and going. It's no wonder that the dream Gideon was listening to was about a loaf of barley bread tumbling into the Midianite camp like a giant boulder. I wonder if the guy who had this dream happened to have watched Indiana Jones the night before. I also wonder what it must have been like to verbalize a dream he had that involved a loaf of barley bread that was larger than life.

Sometimes the details of the dream can seem larger than life and crazy, but if we are willing to listen to others, we realize that we have access to encouragement and empowerment in leadership that helps us take the next step towards victory. While God is waking you up and leading you, make sure to take the time to listen; to Him and to the people that He leads you to. And when you do, I think you won't be able to help but to worship God and to start moving.

I love when I get a chance to go back home and see family. Thankfully, for me, that's not all that far away since I live in the same area where I grew up. Everyone has their camp—the place you can always find yourself able to go back to. It's the place you go to for wisdom, help, and your favorite meal from time to time. It's the people that will go with you no matter the challenge or the situation.

Wherever your camp is that you go back to, it is likely where you will find the people who you are the closest to, the people that believe in you. We often invite those who are closest to us to go with us because of their belief in us. They are the remaining ones out of the many that will go to great lengths to see victory. But our invitation is extended because of our trust and belief in them. They are the vests that help protect us and the resources in our hands that continue to help us in our leadership of others. They help us get mobilized to cross the street with the others that follow behind. There is nothing better than having someone believe in you.

Find the ones who believe in you. Tell them about the dreams that God has given you, and ask them if they would go with you. Asking for help isn't an admission of weakness but an addition of strength. While Gideon probably wondered at certain points what it would have looked like to have 32,000, he could be confident to know and believe in the 300 that remained faithful in his leadership and made his mission their own. Believe in the who that is around you. Sometimes it's getting back to the people that we believe in that helps us be able to get up and go. For Gideon, it was the first thing he said to the Israelite army once he got back. Get up, and let's go do this.

Much of what we've talked about so far has been some of the behind-the-scenes aspects that are experienced when it comes to leadership. If I'm talking in crossing guard terms, it's grabbing the vest and the stop sign, walking to the intersection, taking a look at the traffic situation, and beginning to wait for the people who will need help to cross the street. I haven't actively stepped into what it is I'm doing yet, but I've prepared myself to be ready for that moment. We can have dreams and preparations, but it really will be the doing that makes the difference. A dream stays a dream if nothing is done. It's time to get up and go.

FOLLOWING AND LEADING

If I were to say the word "Wisconsin," near the top of the list of words that would come to mind (other than cheese) would probably be the word winter. We get a lot of it. Our seasons seem to consist of "winter" and "almost winter." One of the perks of our "almost winter" is having birds that perch in trees and sing outside our window. But once the cold starts to come in, those birds head out and move south. For someone who is directionally challenged, I'm always so amazed at the birds that fly over towards warmer weather. As they fly in the V formation, one bird always flies in the front. I wonder how they decide which bird will be selected as the one to lead the flock.

There's a tremendous amount of responsibility that goes along with being the leader. Notice that you can't spell leader without lead. Leadership will require you to be willing to be the first to step out. Some of the greatest responsibility is not only the direction that we are heading in, but knowing that while we are moving, there are people who are following not all that far behind us.

Vulnerable leadership does not only point the way but shows the way. It leads by example. The crossing guard always walks out first to make sure it's safe before the people follow. The bird at the front of the flying V will always be leading the flock. Before he told them to follow his lead, he told them to watch what he was doing. It was so important that Gideon said it to the Israelite army as they were preparing to go into the Midianite camp.

Two of your greatest assets in leadership will always be your communication and your example. The two go hand in hand. Your communication will become the explanation of direction, and your example will become your edge when it comes to executing the plan with precision. Take the time to articulate where you are going and know specifically what to take with you as you do.

Leadership is not only about what you carry in your own hands but also what you put in the hands of others to help them be successful. To us, it would make sense that as Gideon and his army marched into the Midianite camp, they would be fully equipped with swords and shields. But they didn't. Instead of swords and shields, they carried torches inside empty jars and trumpets. Yes, you read that right. Torches and trumpets. Fire and sound. I'm sure the Israelite army had to wonder if they were doing jazz around a campfire more than a Midianite takeover. It may not make sense, but it's exactly the things that you hope are in the hands of the people who follow behind you.

We talked about the two things that are important for a leader to have, and there are two things that are important for a leader to also give and develop in people. The figurative torch and trumpet of leadership to give to people is both passion and a voice.

Fire and sound can do incredible things. Think about how quickly light and noise can captivate your attention, changing the temperature of the atmosphere or drawing you to the attention of its beauty. Illuminating and generating warmth and comfort to the coldest person or place. Time to thank your fire place and your favorite music artist. With the fire of your passion and the sound of your voice, you have the opportunity for those in your camp around you to be able to sense the fire of their passion and the sound of their voice. While these are all great things, there is a flip side to fire and sound. Too much of either of these two things can become dangerous. Fire can create chaos, burning structures down and taking everything in its path. Sound decibels can become so loud that it pierces and ruptures the eardrums. Too much passion at the wrong moment can create chaos and destruction. Too much sound at the wrong moment can become noisy confusion and future misunderstandings. As a leader, make sure you are giving the right amount of kindle to people's fire and the right channel for people's voices to be heard.

MAKE SOME NOISE

Before Gideon and his army moved into the Midianite camp, there was one last unusual thing that was done. You may have, at one point, accidentally done this at a grocery store. I know I have. At the sound of the trumpets, the last thing Gideon's army was told to do was to smash their jars. If I smash a jar, it usually is an accident, and it's only one. Imagine three hundred jars simultaneously being smashed at once. I'm glad I wasn't the clean-up guy. More than just a fun moment, though, this jar smashing feels symbolic.

If you remember before, these empty jars were placed over the top of the torches, likely concealing the fire that burned on the inside. I believe each of us has been given something that we are passionate about. Whether it's going into the Midianite camp or making time to help people cross the street, both are meaningful.

There might be a temporary holding period when you need to put the jar over the fire, but don't let it permanently extinguish the flame. God gave us all something meaningful to offer this world. And because He gives us meaning, He also gives the right timing. Don't let the pressure of what is burning inside get outside of the timing that God has for you. An empty jar smashed at the wrong time can lead to a big mess. Let the jar hold your fire in a time of preparation, and at the right timing, let it be released so that it isn't forever covered in limitations.

If you are waiting to know when to smash your jar, listen for the sound.

I learned a lot of lessons while I held up that stop sign in the middle of the street. I don't know how many countless people I managed to help get from one side to the other each day after school, but I can tell you that each day was equally as important as the next. Leadership likely isn't a one-day deal. It was many days going to the closet at 2:30 p.m., grabbing the vest and stop sign, walking to the early elementary building, and getting people across the street safely. Doing that routine over and over again may have been the greatest lesson I learned that year. No matter what you are leading, stay obedient.

It is obedience that usually leads to purpose and

peace. You may not feel like you are the most gifted or skilled to lead, but you can always make up for it in obedience. And if God calls you like he called Gideon, you can now carry the promise that He is there with you in whatever it is to accomplish. Gideon and the Israelite army ultimately took the territory and experienced victory. Along the way, there were many specific things that God asked Gideon to do before and during the time they crossed into the Midianite camp. These were all steps, but they were simply opportunities to be obedient. It was the obedience of Gideon and his army that made for the opportunity. It was God who caused the outcome.

No matter what opportunity it is that you are led to do, always remember who you are doing it for because He is the one who holds the outcome. Without people walking across the street, my job as a crossing guard would've consisted of just me in the middle of a street, holding up traffic. But with people that God loves and cares for moving safely from one side of the street to the other, it was an opportunity to do something to give glory to God and to benefit people.

Whether it was 32,000 or 300, at the end of the day . . .

It was all for one.

Now, go break some jars and make some noise.

SIDES AND SIGNALS OF VULNERABLE LEADERSHIP

1
Find Focus

8
Make Some
Noise

2
Be Open
in the Quiet

7
Empower
People

3
Listen

6
Take the Lead

4
Believe in the
Who Around You

5
Get Up and Go

CHAPTER ELEVEN

MORE THAN A SURVIVOR
WALKING THROUGH SHADOWS

If there's one person you don't want to take camping with you, it's more than likely me. It's not that I don't like camping. I love the idea of being out in nature. I think there is so much beauty that we can access being in the wonderful work that is God's creation. I'm just really bad when it comes to living in the wild and surviving the elements. Shows like Survivor and Alone entertain me but don't make sense to me. I will be the first to admit that I am a creature of comfort. I like to sleep with the fan on at night. It's my version of a natural breeze. I like waking up with the heat set just right. It's my version of sunrise. I like going to our coffee bar in the morning and putting in a Nespresso pod. It's my version of morning dew. The idea of going into the wild with nothing but a tent, a knife, and a cooler gives me anxiety. Call me domesticated, but there is just something about being in an environment where you are at the mercy of the great outdoors to determine your comfort. Glamping (glamorous camping) is where it's at for me.

While I'm no expert at camping in a physical sense, there is another kind of camping that I have done and can be pretty good at. Some of those mental, emotional, relational, and spiritual dry seasons have been short and other seasons longer, depending on the nature of the situation. Seasons when hurt from other people would cause me to stay hidden in my tent rather than work through the pain. Getting depressing news and disappointing people left me stuck in the desert of what I thought I deserved. Anger and anxiety about what I see in or around me so much to the point I decided to go it alone. Fear and worry led me to deep and dark places. Stress and insecurities left me feeling starved.

These are just a few of the valleys that I know I've spent some time camping in. Maybe you have too. We've been in places internally that have felt like death. If you have managed to get as far as today in your life without having any challenges, I congratulate you and would love to sit down and know how you have done so well, but the chances are that if you are alive and breathing today, you have dealt with the difficulty of a valley. And those challenges we face are nothing new. They go all the way back to the Garden of Eden.

No one is exempt from difficulty in life. Some of the people we consider the strongest and the greatest in all of history have had their own time in the valley. Valleys we know about and others that we don't. Thankfully for us, a king took some time and wrote about his own valley to help us know how to navigate through ours. The Bible calls it Psalm 23. For the sake of this chapter, though, let's call it your Valley of the Shadow of Death Survivor Guide. Before we get started, though, let's agree that whatever valley, no matter how dark or deep it has been or is right now, has a way out. Some of the steps may not be easy, but still possible. You may get tempted to stay where you are, but with some vulnerability and availability to take those steps, however small they may feel, you will be able to walk out of the darkness of the valley and into the light and a fuller picture.

Are you ready?

VALLEY REALITY

Some of you might have been able to put together the clues of Psalm 23 and a king and know who I'm about to talk about. But for those who maybe still don't know (and that's perfectly okay), the shepherd boy turned king and writer of Psalm 23 that I'm talking about is none other than David. Most of you probably remember David for his most iconic moment of slaying Goliath via your Sunday School flannelgraph lesson or through a sports symbol for one team being a huge under-dog against another. That moment doesn't seem like much of a valley. That actually seems pretty awesome if you ask me. You don't have to be insanely competitive to know that it's nice to win. For David's life, though, it wasn't all flannelgraph champion and future sports references. He experienced some dark days. So much that this chapter would get way too long trying to explain everything in detail. So here are the

CliffNotes.

+ Lived the life of an outlaw on the run due to the jealousy of King Saul, David's predecessor as king.

+ Saw a married woman named Bathsheba on a roof bathing and decided to sleep with her, and she became pregnant.

+ Did not want the husband of Bathsheba, Uriah, to find out David slept with her, so David had him killed.

+ Experienced the death of his child with Bathsheba.

+ His son Amnon is murdered by his other son Absalom.

+ His son Absalom attempts to take the throne from David.

+ His son Absalom is murdered.

+ David deals with a deadly plague that kills many of his people.

If there was anyone who could understand the feeling of the valley of the shadow of death, it was David. While not everything that we have walked through in life is comparable to David's situation, we've known what it's like to experience fear, poor decisions, loss, grief, and pain. For as much as David dealt with, his poetic words seem to have much more power when he writes,

> "Even though I walk through the valley of the shadow of death." Psalm 23:4

The reality is that we will find ourselves in the valley at some point. Poor decisions will be made, people will hurt you, you likely will hurt someone at some point, and the unexpected and uncontrollable will make life just downright hard. No one likes to be in the valley, and yet some decide to stay there. Thinking that staying in the darkness of their despair keeps them from the further disappointment of false hope for light. Not exactly the most encouraging news you have read in this book so far. But keep reading.

Being in the valley leaves us with a choice. Seeing the reality of where you are can begin the journey out of the valley. What you think will always be doesn't have to be forever. The beauty is that at the bottom of the valley, you can turn the situations that you think will be always so into even though. How do you turn your always so into even though?

LET'S GO FOR A WALK

My wife and I try to take our pug Groot out for a walk at least three times a week. Pugs tend to get pudgy pretty quickly, so we walk him so that we don't end up having a dog that looks like a blimp with four legs. Groot loves to go for walks. He loves them so much that if we even say the word walk in a completely unrelated way, he will still run to the door and change our plans for the next twenty minutes. So, we leash him up and head out.

I'm still convinced that we aren't taking our dog for a walk but that he is actually walking us. Remember the game Red Light, Green Light? When someone said, "green light," you would try to run as fast as you could from one side to the other, and when they said, "red light," you had to stop. Our walk with Groot often feels like an intense game of Red Light, Green Light. Every tree, fire hydrant, and patch of grass stepped on by another dog becomes our paused investigation and possibly a yellow graffiti tag, if you know what I mean. Once what smells is all clear, Groot immediately goes on a high-speed chase to the next tree. The unpredictable pace that he wants to go around the block versus the pace we are going makes for a struggle and a sore arm in the end.

Walks like the one I go on with Groot might feel like some of the walks you've been on in the valley. The intense stop and go of emotions, progress, and setbacks, can create quick frustrations when you're trying to turn the corner. You've probably faced some form of all these but make the decision to keep walking. Walking out often requires walking through. You may need to stop for a moment to catch your breath. You may make some progress and take a moment to celebrate. You may have a setback and have to reevaluate. All those things are okay. God has patience in your pace.

Whatever you do, in the middle of your valley, don't make the decision to set up camp. It's easy when we are feeling like death and see a long-heated walk ahead, to dig a hole and call it home. I've felt the temptation to do that plenty of times. That hole in the valley of death can become darker than what was already there. Make the decision to keep walking, even if you have to walk slowly. Dark and unfamiliar territory usually will make you slow down. A small step is still a step. One step closer out of the valley and into freedom. It was true for David. He wrote about it. It's true for Groot. He decides to keep going. He wanted to walk. It can be true for you and me. It's easy to decide to put our head down and stay stuck when we feel like things aren't moving fast enough. Don't let the valley of the shadow of death start to feel like home. You don't have to become a tenant. God has a better place for you.

When Groot and I go for a walk, it doesn't take much to convince him that I am with him. All he has to see is the leash that he is attached to that I'm holding in my hand to know I'm there. When he's on the leash, Groot is pretty fearless. He isn't fazed by the pack of larger dogs on our route or the dogs perched up on their living room couches, barking through the window, baiting him to bark back. He just keeps walking. Maybe it's Groot, but if there ever was a sense of danger, I like to think he would run back to me instead of trying to handle it on his own. Groot doesn't let the fear of evil keep him from walking the path. The next part of David's Psalm tells us we don't have to either. It's also the third part of our valley of the shadow of death survival guide.

"I will fear no evil, for you are with me."
Psalm 23:4

Being able to physically see someone walking with you can feel like a far cry from knowing God is there but not always being able to see Him with you. Especially in the valley. We can think that God is only reserved for the mountains, but for someone who went through what David did and can still believe that God is with Him gives us hope that God does do life with us. Even in the valley.

One of our greatest encouragements we can know is that God is with us even at our worst. One of our greatest motivations is that God is also with us to help us get back to our best. Our greatest sense of danger is not always what it is that we are facing, but the fact that we believe we are facing it alone.

The unfortunate part is that evil does exist. For every hero, there can be a villain. For every good, there can be evil. There is an enemy of God. And that enemy's greatest lie is to convince you that you are alone. Sometimes we buy that lie. So how do we get ourselves out of believing that we are alone?

Sometimes it's hard to see that God is closely next to you when you are walking in the dark. When I'm in the dark and don't know if anyone's there, I start channeling my inner sloth from Goonies and say, "Hey, you guys!"

Your voice is a valuable tool. You can get the attention

of most people within earshot of you just by using a little volume. How much more easily can you get the attention of God, who is with you in the valley, when you call out to Him? It takes vulnerability to ask for help. Knowing God is with you doesn't always mean you quickly get out of the valley, but it does mean you can have more joy as you are walking through the valley. He was always available, but when you choose to be vulnerable, you can see it. Even in the dark.

VOICE IN THE VALLEY

Maybe you still are uncertain or even unconvinced that God is with you in your walk through the valley. And that's okay. We realize the reality of the valley. I hope to get to experience a valley someday. I'm not talking about an internal one because let's be honest, no one goes looking for those. I'm talking about a literal valley.

One of the most well-known valleys is called Death Valley. It's known for its extremes in both dryness and heat. How fitting. Sounds like an ideal vacation plan. The first thing on my checklist when I get there would be to yell at the top of my lungs and see how far my voice can carry. Sound carries further in a valley. As the sound moves from your mouth, it begins to bounce and cascade off the rocks around you and carries your echo further than you could do on your own.

In the valley, it can become easy to believe that you have moved farther away from God and are closer to what is evil. Even if God seems far away, still call out and let your voice carry while you're in the valley. Use the valley to your advantage and take the opportunity to project what it is that you can't seem to see. It's harder to go alone. It's better to go together. And when you do, you can begin to know that God is with you, will shed some light on the shadow of evil, and shepherd you through. Don't go it alone.

David may have become a king, but he didn't start out as one. His initial profession was a shepherd. Not exactly a luxury job. Smelly and low-paying. David still walked away with some valuable lessons that he carried with him long after he left the shepherding business. It also helps us with the last point of our valley of the shadow of death survival guide when he says,

"Your rod and your staff, they comfort me."
Psalm 23:4

I will be the first to tell you that I'm not a shepherd. At least not in a literal sense. I've experienced life without Groot on the leash, and, let me tell you, it's rough. The last time he managed to get off the leash while I wasn't looking, it took an hour and a half of a mile to scoop him up. To him, it's a game. To me, it's a nightmare. You can hear the fear in my voice while I negotiate with him to come back.

David knew what it was like to have to herd sheep back to safe places. He was probably way calmer and more collected than I was with Groot. Notice that David isn't talking about being the shepherd, though. In this sense, he's talking about being the sheep. The shepherd he is speaking of is a shepherd greater than him. God actually speaks of himself as being the good shepherd and knowing how to take care of His sheep. And He has the tools to back it. For Groot and me, it's a leash. For God and David (and us), it's a rod and staff. If God is carrying a rod and staff, they must be important and helpful to us on our journey through the valley.

These two items provide two things in our walk through the valley. The rod provides correction, and the staff provides direction. You can expect both of these to be used when you're vulnerably walking through the valley. Let's talk about the rod for a second. One of the reasons we can know that we don't have to fear evil is because God carries a rod. It's reassuring for us to know He's with us, but also that He's using the rod to go full Rambo and put predators in their place and keep us safe. That's a part of it, but it's not all of it.

The other use of the rod is to keep us in place. It can be the reason why we choose not to call on Him in the first place. Is God hitting you while you're down? No. Just like sheep, we tend to get unruly. Sometimes we prolong our journey in the valley because we are unruly. It's not always intentional. It's often emotional. And it's definitely due to the fact that we like to have control.

We can get good at hitting ourselves while we're down. The difference is when God does it, it provides us with the right direction. There can be pain that comes with that correction. The pain is caused by us because we chose a way that wasn't best for us. Walking it on our own usually takes us to darker places that we didn't want to be in the first place. That correction is what keeps us from further destruction later. God corrects because He knows His way is better. The best part is that He doesn't just point the way, but He will show the way. Being vulnerable in the valley will usually lead to a moment of course correction. God is a gentleman and will always be there with you. He will also give you the free will to choose to go it alone. Choose to take the correction. It may hurt in the moment, but you'll be grateful for the hurt you avoid, the time you save, and for finding what is better.

While God uses the rod to correct, He also uses the staff to direct. Have you ever tried to follow directions in the dark? Try it sometime. I can imagine you now, trying to build Ikea furniture in complete darkness. Weird analogy, but you get the point. It's hardest to have direction when everything seems dark. In your valley, that's what God uses the shepherd's staff for. I can be a bit directionally challenged. I know the five-mile radius that surrounds my house like the back of my hand. One wrong turn outside of that five-mile radius can take me to places I've never seen before. I'm pretty heavily GPS-reliant. The staff is God's positioning system. The difference between myself and God in my valley is that He knows the best way out.

The unusualness of the valley can lead me to wonder where I am. I can wander around for a long time and somehow manage to find a way out. David is convinced his way is better. I am too. The difference between taking God's route instead of my own is trusting. Trusting takes vulnerability. My own journey likes to try and cut corners and shave time off my trip. That couldn't be truer in the valley. Cutting corners in the valley can lead to creating more danger. They call Him a good shepherd for a reason. Our way can go astray, so it's best to let God lead the way. The beauty is that, when you do, it's just another indication that He's right there with you.

VALUE IN THE VALLEY

My walks with Groot can be challenging from time to time. Sometimes, I have to use his harness to pull him back from going into the neighbor's yard. Other times, I need to harness the power of his leash to keep him from going too far or tell him it's time to move on from the tree he is investigating. Despite all of the correcting and directing, I'm grateful, and I know he is too when we get a chance to go around the block. His smile and tongue sticking out can confirm. Believe it or not, I think you can have the same smile by the time you come to the end of the valley. Not just because you got through it, but because of what you found while you were in it.

When you let God lead you, you can find value in your valleys. You realize that it wasn't all life lost, but there were lessons that were learned. We never want to be in valleys, but life has them. I pray that what you've gone through can become the lessons that you can carry into the next journey through the valley. As I've taken the same path with Groot for our walks, different mile markers have been burned into my brain that tells me how close I am to home. The next journey may be different, but the lessons can help the same.

David went through some incredibly difficult seasons in his life, and yet he's mentioned as being a man after God's own heart. You might look at that laundry list of dirt and disappointments and wonder how that's even possible. What qualifies you as being after God's heart is not that you always get everything right, but always knowing and choosing who you can come back to when you don't. I'm thankful that David was vulnerable about his valleys. I'm even more thankful that my valley doesn't have to be my finality. And it doesn't have to be yours either. Don't set up camp in your valley. Keep walking and know you aren't alone. With God, you lack nothing, and He is ready to go on the walk with you.

One more chapter to go, but for right now, it looks like a good time to take Groot for a walk.

CHAPTER TWELVE

VULNERABLE AND VICTORIOUS
FINISHING THE RACE

It was 2004. I stood at the starting line with what felt like a
thousand other people my age who were hungry to be the first
to cross the finish line. It was really more like sixty. Yet there
I stood, palms sweating and legs ready for the sound of the
voice on the bullhorn from Heaven, ready to unleash the pack
of stallions out of the gate. I wasn't worried about finishing. I
was worried about winning. As I heard the countdown from
the man above, I finally saw the light go green in my mind as
he said that one powerful word.

Go.

I remember tearing out in what felt like a flash of lighting.
I was sure that I had left everyone else coughing in the dust
I created. As my legs furiously moved one in front of the
other, I couldn't believe it. For one second, I looked out of the
corner of my eyes to see what felt like every single person was
ahead of me. I was too afraid to look behind me out of fear

that there would be nobody besides the crowd. There's nothing exciting about saying the only people you beat in a race were the ones sitting in the bleachers. My vision of standing on the podium and receiving my gold medal quickly began to fade.

I kept running, and by the time I crossed the finish line, the kids who finished first were already headed to the car with their parents. Did I forget to mention to you that this was my eighth-grade cross country meet? Anyways, after the race was finished, I remember grabbing my paper trophy in the form of a participation ribbon and heading to my mom, dejected and also committed to never run cross country again. Aside from the 5K fundraiser that I get peer-pressured into doing by friends, to this day, I've stuck to the commitment I made all those years ago.

While I might not be putting on the shorts and a running bib (They couldn't come up with a better name for that?), there is another race that I am running. Chances are, if you are reading this, you are running this race too. We woke up this morning with breath in our lungs, blood flowing through our veins, and we get to both run and celebrate this race called life. There is so much beauty along the route of this race. We talked about much of it in the previous chapters of this book—the ability to have access to deeper faith, life-giving friendships and relationships, a bright future, and living in freedom. When these are happening, we feel like we are moving fast. The terrain feels smooth.

As much as we love the easiness of moving on smooth terrain, life can sometimes feel more like hurdles with a heavy incline. The aspects of the race that bring beauty to our lives, are also those that can become our challenges. The challenge of having faith when we are weak, navigating friendships when they become life-taking, finding the brightness in life when it feels dim, and accessing freedom when we feel tied in our circumstances. When those challenges come, any movement can feel as slow as a sloth stuck in molasses.

The good part is that as slow as we may feel we are moving, we are still moving. Life is good at reminding us about how we wish we were going faster than we are. Going fast can lead to us forgetting what we were supposed to take with us all along. We might be at different mile markers in this race, and that's okay. This chapter isn't about trying to get to where we are headed quicker but about what to take with us while we're headed there. What we take can end up being what keeps us going no matter what terrain we are on. We are keeping a good pace, but let's pause for just a second. Life is short enough to keep running and long enough to take a moment to reflect.

Every long race has an aid station at some point along the way. Take a moment with me and stop at the aid station. Get a drink of water. Tie your shoes if the laces start to feel like they are coming loose. The aid you receive at the station may be exactly what you need for the next leg of the race.

RACE RESOURCE

When you think about what you are going to take with you on your race, there are some things you take without question and things that are clearly out of the question. A good pair of running shoes. Clothes that make you more aerodynamic. An anchor.

Wait. Did he just say an anchor? Clearly, that must be in the out of question category.

In a real race, you're right. No way are we tying an anchor to our ankles and expecting to finish. In this race called life, though, this anchor keeps us going. Before you call it quits on this chapter and me crazy, let me tell you why this anchor is important.

The reasons we keep waking up and running this race called life are often twofold. One is the hope that we are making a difference. Hoping we are having an influence and making an impact in the lives of others as well as our own. That each step is helping lead the way for someone who will eventually be where we are.

The other reason we keep running is the hope that life can be different. The belief that if we keep running, we will get to the places of having an influence and making an impact. You don't put hope in what you have already run. You put hope in what is ahead. Hope is a large part of why we run. So what does hope have to do with having an anchor? One of my favorite verses will make that a little clearer.

"We have this hope as an anchor for the soul, firm and secure"
Hebrews 6:19

Anchors are heavy. Try lifting one once. Toss one to a friend. Actually, don't do that. It'll probably end in a hospital visit. You get the point, though. The function of an anchor is to keep some of the largest objects from drifting away. It's easy in life to start to drift away, especially when you don't have the right things keeping you in place. That drifting can begin to feel like the deteriorating of what you hold closest to you. Nothing can get much closer than your soul. Your soul needs an anchor. We have put our hope in and anchored ourselves into things that ultimately don't bring us stability and certainty. They become the anchors that we carry with us that wear us down and cause us to drift in this race called life. It might be time to pull anchor on what makes our hope temporary and drop anchor into what can make our hope become permanent. Fortunately for us, there is an anchor for that because there is a person for that.

Jesus has been called many names. God. Prince of Peace. Jehovah. You could see how long this could get. There are books that are dedicated just to talking about the names of Jesus. He's got a lot of them. He even has one that has to do with running. Right after it talks about hope as an anchor, Jesus gets called another name.

"Our forerunner."

Maybe you needed to look up what that means. I did too. A forerunner is someone who comes before the coming or development of someone or something. The way I think of it best is to call it a "beforerunner." Jesus is our beforerunner. The reason we can have this hope is because Jesus went before us and got it for us. Jesus ran this race 2000 years ago when He came to earth and put His whole life into it. He ran His race perfectly so that we could benefit from the prize that waits for us at the end of our race. Hope is the result of Him.

We can anchor ourselves in Him because He's completed the race on earth that we are currently running. Follow Jesus in your race, and I believe it will bring hope to your race. We don't always know what will happen in our life, but we know who we can take hold of in our life. Taking ahold of this hope and anchoring yourself to it can become the difference between not continuing the race and finishing the race. The firmness of the anchor helps you become an unstoppable force. The security of this anchor helps you have longevity.

CHOOSE YOUR SHOES

Have you ever worked on a project (some companies actually call them sprints), and you start to begin to see the finish line? I feel that with this book. This book has been two years in the making. Somedays, I've felt eager to wake up and get to the computer to let the pages run, one after the other. Other days, I've been winded and felt like I might never see the finish line. And other times when I just wanted to drop out altogether. As I've been writing the final few chapters of this book, I've been encouraged and excited about the opportunity to release this work in the world. The hope is that this would be an encouragement to those who read it. The finish line can be exciting. We all dream of those days when we can lift our arms at the top of the stairs like Rocky Balboa, but it's in each day before that moment that allows us to get there. Hope helps us to keep going because of the belief in what is to come.

One of the most important things to have right when you are in a race is your shoes. Nobody wants to run barefoot in a race. Especially if the race is run through any trails. If hope is one of the shoes you put on in your race of life, the other shoe is perseverance. You can try and run with one shoe, but you probably won't run better without the other. Avid runners know that mile two feels very different from mile twelve. Unless you are running in a circle, the finish line usually isn't found where the starting line began. Perseverance will be needed to help you go the distance. Not too much further ahead in Hebrews, we find the importance of perseverance.

"And let us run with perseverance the race marked out for us, fixing our eyes on Jesus, the pioneer and perfecter of faith."
Hebrews 12:1-2

Running is really just putting one foot in front of the other. Perseverance is the foot that follows in front of hope, and hope is the foot that follows after perseverance. One foot after the other, to create a rhythm and pace to your race. Perseverance helps hope, and hope helps perseverance. If hope is the motivation to keep going, then perseverance is the choice to remain disciplined in the day-to-day of the race. For someone who likes to see the finish line come faster, this is hard. As much as putting one foot in front of the other will get us places, it doesn't mean that it won't feel mundane. Try running in the country or a desert. It gets tough, when every step you take just seems to lead you to the scenery that looks the same. Hope can start to fade when the scenery is the same and the finish line is nowhere in sight. It's easy for life to become a one-legged race when hope starts to fade, and all you have left to go on is perseverance. When that happens, don't fixate on where you are, but get fixed on who the race is for.

ONE RACE TO WIN THEM ALL

One of the principles I've learned in life is to never assume anything about anyone. Especially someone I've never met who is reading a book I wrote. Okay, I added that last part, but still. Someone may have given you this book because they felt like this would be a good resource for the season of life you are in. I hope it has, and thank your friend on behalf of me for thinking that. Maybe you found it on a bookshelf and decided to give it a chance. I know there were many other books you could have picked, but thank you for choosing this one, and I hope it's done something significant for and in your life.

All throughout this book, we've talked about another book—The Bible. I don't know what Jesus means to you. He could (and I believe He wants to be) your savior. He might be (and I believe He is) a good teacher. For you He could be what you say after you badly hurt yourself. Jesus could be two or even all three of those things for you, and much more, or nothing more. Regardless of where you're at, let me offer you a thought of why you might want to consider Him when it comes specifically to your race.

We all have our eyes set on some kind of prize. In a real race, the prize is usually a medal and the pride of finishing first. In life, we often run with the prize of popularity, importance, richness, status, and endless amounts of other reasons. I think our real reason we run those races is because we believe these medals are what will give us what we really want, which is peace and joy.

I'm not here to criticize anyone who has or is running that race. I've run those same things, and I realized something when I ran them—there is no real finish line. When we run the race for those prizes, we usually think of our finish line as the person that is ahead of us that we want to surpass. But what happens, and where do you go when you race past everyone you're chasing after? When I tried, it may have left me with feeling the pride of the prize, but no real peace or happiness. None of those things brought about satisfaction or perfection because none of them could ever get me the full distance. It's like running to what you think is a finish line, and when you're about to cross it, the finish line moves again. My faith in those prizes began to disappoint. Hoping for a medal and, instead, getting a participation ribbon.

Jesus isn't just a savior or a good teacher. He is the reward. He is the reward because He ran it and because He ran it perfectly. He is the pioneer who has gone before us, faithfully and perfectly ran the race, and therefore knows the finish line. I can't consult with the prizes of popularity and richness that have no finish line. That race has no destination, just a lot of competition and comparison. I can consult with the one who crossed the finish line. When you fix your eyes, you can know there is a finish and that it will end with Him.

I think peace and joy are really what we consider perfection. He happens to be the fullness of both of those. He has enough to give to everyone. The cost to run perfectly what no one else could was great. It wasn't a walk through the park but a journey that led to the pain of a cross.

We aren't doing it perfectly even after Jesus finished His race on earth and headed back home to Heaven. And despite that, when we run towards Him, He stands at the finish line, cheering us on. He ran the race and hands us the reward. The one who is perfect is worth hoping in and persevering toward.

Life feels like a sprint but should be run like a marathon. You can run so fast in this life that you don't get to appreciate what you see while you're running. This race has no ranking. The best part in knowing that is that you don't have to feel the pressure to move at the pace that everyone else says you need to go, but can move at the pace that God has set for you. As long as you finish, you get first place. In God's race, victory isn't about being the best but about finishing what you started with Him. You may not feel like you are quite where everyone else is, and the journey may feel a bit bumpy. The run through the rough terrain makes us have a greater appreciation for the smooth terrain. Each of the races we run are important. Your race matters.

Keep hoping.

Keep persevering.

Keep perspective.

Keep putting one foot in front of the other.

And when you run in His direction, there is victory waiting for you.

FINAL THOUGHTS

This book started on the living room couch at the beginning of 2020, which most of us know as the year of Covid. Interesting how a year that uses the numbers to tell someone they have perfect vision became the numbers many are trying to forget. For many, it's the year they have felt their vision pause or even end. I didn't know where all these words would lead, but I knew I needed a place to create and have a vision for something while it seemed like the world stopped. As much as I wrote this book to hopefully help meet someone's need, I didn't realize how much it would meet my own need. I've probably learned more than I've given over the course of these two years of on and off writing.

This book has been a journey. If I can be vulnerable with you, as I've been writing this, I've battled feelings of insecurity. I've dealt with anxious thoughts and the fear of failure. I've spent more time wondering if I am just wasting my time writing this than if this would cause someone to come alive with wonder all over again. It wasn't easy, and somehow, with God's help, here we are. In the midst of my own realities, I have been able to experience victory. Some of the victories were already there, and some that I now see are new to me.

I still feel like a rough draft in process. Some of these victories that I have been able to find have been put on the pages to become the victory that I hope you can see. Vulnerability tends to breed vulnerability. I may not have lived as much life as many of the writers out there, but I figured it was time to get vulnerable and real about the reality of life. It's interesting how the vulnerability of others in their journey can encourage me to know I can be vulnerable and have victory too.

I may not know all of what you are going through, but I hope sharing some of my most vulnerable moments with you helps you feel like you have someone you can relate to. I've experienced the struggles of faith, the tension in friendship, doubts about the future, and the felt lack of freedom. I've tried to act like I have it all together. It takes way more effort to try to always be right than it is to be real. We can try to pretend to be something, but then do we really have victory? Can there be victory without vulnerability? It's the question that started this journey. Victory begins at the ending of pretending. Congratulations on finishing this book and I hope as you have read this, you felt encouraged to be vulnerable and will experience the ability to be victorious.

NOTES

CHAPTER 1: REALITY UNDER THE RUG
1. John 10:10
2. Genesis 3:1-7
3. Genesis 2:16-17
4. Genesis 3:3
5. Luke 19:10

CHAPTER 2: THE VOICE OF VULNERABILITY
1. John 14:1
2. John 14:6

CHAPTER 3: RECIPE FOR CLARITY
1. Psalm 34:8
2. Matthew 7:7
3. Matthew 4:18-19
4. Matthew 20:28

CHAPTER 4: THAT ONE THING
1. Romans 7:15
2. Matthew 26:69-75
3. Matthew 26:74-75
4. John 21:1-3
5. John 21:15-19
6. Proverbs 26:11

CHAPTER 5: FACING FAITH
1. Hebrews 11:1
2. Matthew 14:22-33

CHAPTER 6: FRIEND WITH NO END
1. Andy Stanley Quote
2. Luke 5:17-26
3. 1 Corinthians 15:33
4. Luke 5:20
5. Luke 5:26

CHAPTER 7: GROWING FUTURE
1. Matthew 7:24-27
2. Romans 5:4

CHAPTER 8: FINDING FREEDOM
1. John 16:33
2. John 8:31-32

CHAPTER 9: LICENSED AND DETERMINED
1. Judges 6:11-12
2. Judges 6:13
3. Zig Ziglar Quote
4. Judges 6:14
5. Judges 6:23

CHAPTER 10: CROSSING THE STREET
1. Judges 7
2. Judges 7:9
3. Judges 7:13
4. Judges 7:17
5. Judges 7:15-17
6. Judges 7:19

CHAPTER 11: MORE THAN A SURVIVOR
1. 2 Samuel 6-13
2. Psalm 23:4

CHAPTER 12: VULNERABLE AND VICTORIOUS

1. Hebrews 6:19
2. Hebrews 6:20
3. Hebrews 12:1-2

ABOUT THE AUTHOR

Zach Mueller currently serves as a Campus Pastor for Poplar Creek Church in Greenfield Wisconsin helping people know how much God loves Greenfield. Zach is a graduate from North Central University and married to his wife Rachel since 2017. He has a passion for people to discover the full life they have been looking for. Zach has had opportunities to speak at and serve in many different schools, retreats, conferences and prisons.

If you are currently a leader of any Church, school, business or event and would like to contact Zach to come and speak, you can email him at zachm@poplarcreek.org and he would be happy to connect with you. Just be prepared that he may claim to be the world's biggest Dr. Pepper fan.

Made in the USA
Monee, IL
21 August 2024

64257131R00104